CHART S

A guide to processing the inforn
living workable part o:

CHART SYNTHESIS

Applied Interpretation
in Natal Astrology

by

Roy Alexander
B.Sc., D.F.Astrol.S.

THE AQUARIAN PRESS
Wellingborough, Northamptonshire

First published 1984

© ROY ALEXANDER 1984

British Library Cataloguing in Publication Data

Alexander, Roy
   Chart synthesis.
   1. Horoscopes   2. Astrology
   I. Title
   133.5'4   BF1728.A2

ISBN 0-85030-364-8

The Aquarian Press is part of the Thorsons Publishing Group

Printed and bound in Great Britain by
Whitstable Litho Ltd., Whitstable, Kent

CONTENTS

PREFACE

This book is intended as a practical guide to organizing the material that is generated by interpreting an astrological chart. It is therefore also a bridge between interpretation and counselling and offers some guidance in both of those areas so that the process of interpretation-synthesis-counselling can be seen as a whole.

Most of the book, however, consists of working through charts in detail, using several systems of organizing the material. The reader thus has the opportunity of deciding which way of doing it is most suited to his own needs — which may vary from client to client. Students should become familiar with all the systems presented here so that they can develop a flexible approach to the use of astrology, rather than being stuck in a particular pattern.

To become really effective astrologers, we need to know what factors in the chart mean at a level of feeling and experience. Many students make the mistake of not going beyond a purely intellectual grasp of delineations and, indeed, most of the books available encourage such an attitude implicitly by never mentioning the issue. For most of us, the intellectual grasp has to come first and so books of standard delineations give us an invaluable starting-point. One of my objects in this book, however, is to discuss astrological symbolism in such a way that its underlying structure becomes readily accessible, so that the reader can use this structure to go beyond the intellectual understanding of the meanings of planets, signs and houses to an integrated *experience* of their meanings.

The problem of sexist pronouns seems to become especially acute in writing such a book as this. Unfortunately, until there is general agreement on some neutral form, there is no satisfactory solution to the difficulty. Using s/he or 'him or her' all the time soon becomes contrived. In the interests of maintaining a readable prose style, I have for the most part followed the prevailing convention of using the masculine form to refer interchangeably to either sex.

1.
SYNTHESIS AND THE NATURE OF ASTROLOGY

Learning to *interpret* a birth chart is relatively easy — at least to a first level of competence. I used to teach astrology at evening classes and I found that over a period of ten or twelve weeks anyone who was committed to it could start from scratch and become a reasonably accurate, if rather hesitant, chart interpreter. Of course, it takes more like two or three years of intensive study and practice to become really fluent, but it is not nearly as difficult as it looks to acquire some measure of basic skill — especially with the number of clear interpretation texts that are available now.

The trouble is that when we interpret a chart we get a mass of information, some of it repetitious, some of it contradictory. This information then needs to be synthesized in such a way that it can be presented to a client, either face to face or on paper. And this is where it starts to get difficult. The astrologer is inclined to be overwhelmed by the mass of material. It is bad enough just with the basic chart. If we want to take into account midpoints, asteroids, Arabian parts and harmonics, the situation is even worse.

The problem is not in any lack of systems for organizing the material. In fact, a common way of tackling the difficulty is to set up a number of categories and classify the information in terms of them. There is the Margaret Hone method of dividing it up into more or less arbitrary categories such as love, home, friends, health and so on. Another method is to take the houses as experiences of life and interpret the chart round the clock, taking into consideration the sign on the cusp, the ruler of that sign and planets in the house. We can do it by order of the planets, taking into account sign, house position and aspects. Or we can use a weighting system, giving or withholding points for such matters as planets in own signs or houses, stress on elements or qualities, etc.

All these systems have their merits as means of *displaying*

information but none of them actually synthesizes the material and
much of the current confusion about chart synthesis arises from the
mistaken notion that they do.

The purpose of this book is to present a practical working method
of handling chart synthesis; but in order to do that, we need to spend
some time looking at the basic issues involved in what we are doing.
This includes taking a look at the nature of astrology itself. One of
the major problems in the practice of astrology is that we leave
unresolved all sorts of fundamental questions about its nature. These
questions then come back to haunt us in a very practical way when
we are actually engaged in the work: for example, you may find yourself
saying almost the same things to different clients with different charts
and wondering how on earth you would justify this if challenged; giving
accurate information from a chart that subsequently turns out to be
wrong; having a client reject completely an obvious and major theme
in the chart. These things may not at first sight seem to have much
to do with chart synthesis but they are at the very heart of the problem.

Let us start with a dictionary definition of synthesis: 'Combination
of separate parts, elements, etc. into a whole or into a system; that
which results from this process.' The crucial part of that definition
is 'into a whole or into a system'. The difficulties that arise when we
are thinking about chart synthesis are a consequence of the fact that
we are usually only thinking in terms of half of the system — the
astrologer's half. As a matter of fact, the astrologer alone cannot
synthesize a chart. The information is only synthesized when it becomes
a living and workable part of the client's experience. People who write
about synthesis tend to assume that it can be done without the
participation of the client and to lose sight of the reality that we are
really dealing with the system astrologer-chart-client. The chart is
synthesized when the information increases a client's awareness and
makes a difference in the way in which he thinks about himself, be
it in deep psychological terms or in ordinary everyday terms, depending
on what the client needs or can handle.

What the astrologer can do is to present the material in such a way
as to facilitate the client's expanded awareness of himself. Any of the
systems of organizing the material that I have mentioned earlier can
be used. However, part of what I will be suggesting in this book is
that the material itself should be allowed to create its own categories
and so organize itself into about half a dozen basic themes and perhaps
into one overall theme which summarizes the entire chart.

To put it in slightly different words, the astrologer's job is to make
the chart information become real for the client, to take him beyond a

merely intellectual agreement with the information that is given. Obviously, this statement immediately opens up a divide between mail-order work and face-to-face work. With mail-order work, about all we can do is to state the basic themes of the chart as clearly as possible. We can perhaps give some general guidelines as to how the client might use the information and we will be looking at that possibility later. With face-to-face work, we can go a good deal further and encourage the client to discuss the chart themes and relate them to his or her actual life.

The main thing to remember at this stage is that the client's state of mind, capacity for recognizing and accepting personal information and resistance to change are vital factors in the synthesis of a chart. Indeed in any given case perhaps the most that we can do is just present information organized to the best of our ability.

Some of what I am saying will seem to be slightly at odds with a lot of other books. For the most part, astrologers and astrological writers tend to talk and write as though interpretation were an end in itself. This leads, as I have said, to some very basic questions about the nature of astrology being ignored, with resulting difficulties in actually using astrology.

It is rather as though psychological tests, such as the Rorschach or IQ tests, were used as ends in themselves rather than as means to ends. If we imagine an entire sub-culture of people doing Rorschach and IQ tests on each other and writing books and having conferences about them without much more than a vague nod in the direction of the purpose of all this activity, this would not be an unfair analogy with the present state of astrology. This unhealthy state of affairs actually prevents astrology from being practised as effectively as it could be.

So before we move on to the practical details of organizing chart information, let us try to get some sense of what astrology is really about and to take a look at some of our assumptions about it. And the reason we need to do this is to manifest some of the conflicts and confusion that hinder our ability to synthesize a chart, not for the sake of an abstract discussion, interesting though that might be.

There are, broadly, two ways of coming at astrology. One is the psychic approach. Some people use the chart merely as a stimulus to their own psychic faculties, as a link with the person they are doing the reading for. Often such people need only a minimal knowledge of astrology and they may barely be able to set up a chart properly. If you have those sort of abilities, this approach can and does work but it is a form of clairvoyance, rather than astrology in the sense in which it is being discussed in this book. I do not mean to put down this approach but they are rare individuals whose clairvoyant powers are totally reliable. The impressions they receive are filtered through their own systems of beliefs and perceptions and thus interpreted according to the particular bias of the practitioner. Nevertheless, accurate information can be obtained from the chart in this manner. Astrology is weird! That simple statement is the key to a lot of issues. Astrology is very, very weird stuff indeed. But, there is another side to astrology and those of us who follow mainly the second approach described below tend to get hooked on the seemingly rational aspect of the subject.

The second approach is the one used in this book and most other books, articles and lectures on astrology. It assumes that a chart can be interpreted by a set of definable rules, that no special psychic ability is necessary and, indeed, that an accurate first approximation of a person's character can be obtained by looking up standardized meanings in an interpretation text. This approach is definitely valid. Not only is it the one that most trained astrological practitioners use but even a computer can be programmed to produce a recognizably accurate portrait from the birth chart. It is true that such portraits are fairly clumsy and crude compared with one produced by a skilled human astrologer, but today's computers are really pretty crude — in fact, about as intelligent as a beetle. However, it is by no means fanciful to think in terms of a future computer sophisticated enough not to merely churn out the meaning of each aspect or sign and house position but also to select and combine information and produce a sensitive and balanced analysis indistinguishable from one produced by a human being. (Not that such a computer would destroy the function of the human astrologer, any more than a computer which could provide an accurate medical diagnosis would do away with the need for doctors to actually heal the patients. Astrology today is like medicine would be if all that doctors did was diagnose.)

So, this second, rational, approach to interpretation can be used by anyone and we can even, at least in theory, look forward to the day when all the work of analysis and organization of the material can be done by computer. Notice I am not calling it 'synthesis'. The synthesis, if it happens at all, happens in the person-to-person counselling after the analytical work has been done. To really harness the power of astrology and turn it into a powerful diagnostic tool completely independent of how the practitioner happens to be feeling that morning seems a desirable goal. And to have astrology as generally acceptable and available as intelligence tests seems even more desirable. So what is preventing this? It is certainly not lack of dedication and effort — rather the hauntings that I mentioned earlier. So let us have a shot at laying these particular ghosts.

The first thing that we need to confront squarely is that astrology is profoundly non-rational (or as I said earlier, 'weird'). It only *looks* as though it could be dealt with rationally and scientifically. Trying to handle it that way works up to a point — enough to lure us into thinking that it really is possible — then we run into the ghosts, the seemingly insoluble contradictions.

There are a number of threads here that we need to pick up carefully if we are to make sense of them. The first is the basic assumption that we have about the nature of the world. We are all living in a general context that the world is somehow 'out there', apart from ourselves, that our consciousness has no effect on it and that the laws of this world and the ways of dealing with it can be discovered by detached, impersonal observation and analysis. In short, we are all enclosed in a fishtank of deeply-held beliefs and assumptions that are to do with the universe being divided into subjective and objective realms. Whether these beliefs and assumptions are true or not, they are what we have to deal with and, as such, they certainly have a sort of interim truth. What needs to concern us here is that, within this kind of fishtank of objectivity, astrology does not really make sense. It works, but it does not make sense. All the ghosts and hauntings that prevent us making full use of astrology arise from our own compulsive need to have it make sense. This 'no-sense' at the very heart of what we are doing is more than inconvenient; it is downright alarming and that makes it difficult to confront. Astrologers basically react to it in one of three ways. The first reaction is that astrology is something mantic and mysterious, not to be subjected to close scrutiny and essentially different from most other human activities. This has the effect of making such astrologers seem like a group of oddballs who need not be taken seriously by the community at large.

The second way of reacting is to strive to prove that astrology *does* make sense. This is what motivates astrological research. The assumption behind such research seems to be that if we can find more information, which we can reduce to statistical statements, then astrology will make sense. Another aspect of this type of reaction (which does not, in fact, seem to be so much discussed these days) is the attempt to produce cause and effect theories of astrology. These, in essence, boil down to the idea that some kind of as yet undiscovered force, electrical or gravitational perhaps, has some kind of yet undiscovered effect on our genes at birth. Such notions completely gloss over the issue of why a planet should have a different effect depending on what part of the sky it was in at the time. Nowadays there is a general tendency to say 'We don't know how astrology works' with the assumption that some day we will.

The third reaction is simply to abandon astrology. A number of potentially good students become involved with astrology and quite skilled, then, because the discipline does not measure up to what they imagine are the necessary criteria of scientific objectivity, they feel increasingly uncomfortable and fraudulent and stop practising. Such people are usually particularly intelligent and sensitive and a severe loss to astrology.

The way to handle this mess is simply to acknowledge that astrology does not make sense in the context of the rational, scientific, objective universe that we seem to live in, and then use it nevertheless. I want it to be especially clear what I am saying here. I am not saying *ignore* the fact that astrology does not make sense; I am saying simply let it be so. Let go of being attached to whether it has to make sense or being defensive about the fact that it does not. There are some very good precedents in other areas (especially mathematics) for this kind of move. Most people will probably have heard of the case of the square root of minus one. If we multiply quantities of the same mathematical sign together, we always get a plus: $+1 \times +1 = +1$; -1×-1 still gives $+1$. So, what figure multiplied by itself gives -1? That question makes no sense at all. You can't even start to grasp it; it has none of the seeming rationality of astrology. Yet the square root of minus one has some very practical applications. The theory of alternating current electrical generators makes heavy use of it. This example illustrates the point that if something works but makes no sense or has anomalies in terms of the context in which it is being used we may need to recognize that it belongs to another context altogether and *to accept it as it is*, not demanding that it fit with the criteria we are familiar with.

As a matter of fact the context of a subjective versus objective universe disappears when it is closely examined. The findings of sub-atomic physics are that the universe has to be considered in terms of the total relatedness of the observer to what he is observing. This is a context in which astrology makes sense, though few astrologers seem to be aware of that. It has not penetrated very far into the mass consciousness as yet, which means that astrologers are rather ahead of their time and not behind it, as some of our critics would maintain.

A major practical consequence of the argument so far is that we have to stop thinking of the birth chart as being something cut and dried, like a chemical formula. For one thing, as we have seen, astrology belongs to a different context or a different dimension. It is the same dimension that particle physics belongs to and we do not really know what the rules of operating in that dimension are yet. One of the things that we *do* know is that the idea of hard and fast cause and effect breaks down. Another thing that we know is that, in order to have things work, we have to consider the whole system. As far as the subject of chart synthesis is concerned this means that we have to consider the astrologer, the chart and the client as a total system, the parts of which interact with each other. This brings us to the issue of counselling, which is the subject of another book in this series. I am not proposing to go into it very deeply but I will have to say something about it in order to put the question of chart synthesis into complete perspective.

Another book in this series deals with chart interpretation and, again, I will do no more than glance at that subject. What I will mainly concentrate on, in the bulk of this book, are practical ways of organizing the interpreted material so as to prepare the way for the synthesis of it within the client's experience. To do this, I will be taking the view that using standardized meanings is valid and we need to look at the arguments involved.

Some astrologers prefer to come at the chart and the client together, with little preliminary study of the chart, relying heavily on intuition and inspiration to produce an accurate interpretation. They argue, and quite rightly, that the same chart factor will not work in exactly the same way in two different people. This is saying, in slightly different words, what I have said above, that we have to consider the astrologer, the chart and the client as a complete system.

The opposite of the intuition and inspiration approach too often consists of reaching into textbook or memory for a standard meaning and then insisting on it, whether or not it is really appropriate to the client. This is especially a tendency among inexperienced astrologers who are still uncertain of their own skills and, indeed, may be still uncertain whether astrology can fully deliver the goods. Such an approach treats astrology as though it were a rational, intellectual exercise — which, as we have seen, it is not — and supposes that chart factors have fixed and definite meanings, as though the chart were a chemical equation that always yields the same result.

There is paradox and confusion here because even the most spontaneous and intuitive astrologer has some definite notion about, say, the Moon in Leo at the back of his head. That notion will coincide broadly with the ideas that other astrologers have about the meaning of Moon in Leo. So do chart factors have definite meanings or not?

To answer this question — and therefore begin to release a lot of blockage on practical interpretation and synthesis — we need to recognize that each chart factor needs to be described and thought about in terms of a wide *spectrum* of meaning. *Any definition that we choose to work with is a selection from that spectrum and it implies the rest of the spectrum.* Jupiter is not Saturn, any more than a dog is a cat. However, there are many breeds of dogs, and there are many breeds of cats. Each animal is firmly rooted in its 'dogness' or 'catness' however little resemblance there may seem to be between individual specimens. A playful kitten and a full grown lion are both cats, though your reactions to them are likely to be very different, especially if the lion is loose! In the same way, there is a whole range of meanings of Jupiter, Saturn, Aries, Pisces and all the other chart factors. It is not a question of some being right and some being wrong but of which ones are appropriate to the job.

Jung's idea of archetypes is useful here. An archetype is not a thing but rather an invisible organizing principle behind a whole category of things. Thus, we might say that there is an archetype of 'catness' which generates things to do with cats — not only actual cats but our thoughts about them, pictures of them and so on. Jung compares the archetype with the invisible potential of the crystal lattice that is present in a saturated solution. It can hardly be said to exist, in the sense in which we normally use the term, yet it organizes the crystals that form within it into very definite shapes.

In the same way, there is an archetype called Jupiter which manifests as such seemingly various phenomena as sports, clergymen, bankers, joviality, philosophy, extravagance and so on. The whole page could be filled with attributes of Jupiter — which we use depends on the results we want. If we and the client are concerned mainly with concrete events, it will be appropriate to use the concrete meanings of Jupiter and other chart factors. If we are concerned with inner processes, we will use the psychological meanings. The one does not exclude the other and, if we are aware of the spectrum of meaning, we can select whichever one is most appropriate to our client.

Although it often does not look that way, the more abstract the meaning the more powerful it is. If a client comes in cursing the intransigence of his bank manager, it will probably be more productive if we can shift the emphasis to the question of his own extravagance. Information that we give to a client sets off a resonance of the entire spectrum related to that information. The client might start off with a problem with the bank manager and end up examining the issue of his faith in God. Giving information from the chart is like putting an electrical potential across a circuit to see how it is working. It lights up the clients' circuits so that we and they can take a better look at them and so give them an opportunity of integrating, or synthesizing them. Again this is, strictly speaking, the province of counselling, which we will look at in a later chapter.

The answer to whether chart factors have definite meanings is that they have definite *ranges* of meanings. Any particular selection from this range will provoke a reaction of some sort in a client, even if it is only bewilderment. As long as we stay alive to the existence of the *range* of meanings and to the fact that a client might be reactivated anywhere in the spectrum, it does not greatly matter which particular meaning we choose to start with. So, you can use your favourite set of delineations, provided you do not insist on those meanings being absolutely definitive. There is all the difference in the world between cramming an interpretation down a client's throat and using it as a basis of discussion.

In practical terms, it is a matter of first defining what we think a client's Venus in Leo in the tenth square Mars, trine Saturn and opposite Pluto means, to take a random example. The second half of the job is using that definition to find out what the client feels about that issue and so illuminate it and create the conditions for synthesis. The more generally the interpretation is phrased the more likely it is to light up the client's circuits. In the next chapter, we will look at interpreting a chart from scratch and organizing the information into a number of general themes, ready for use.

2.
DISCOVERING CHART THEMES (1)

In this chapter we shall consider how to extract coherent basic themes from the mass of material that arises from delineating a chart. First, of course, we need to generate the material. The most useful format for our purpose is to go through the chart planet by planet, making notes on the meanings of sign and house position and aspects. The format is basically that used by Jeff Mayo and Margaret Hone and will be familiar to many readers.

The planets are where the action is in the chart. They are like verbs in sentences. A model that I find useful to keep in mind when doing interpretation (and for which I am indebted to Dane Rudhyar) is that the planet is like an engine that needs a certain type of fuel to run on (the sign) and certain types of circumstances to operate in (the house). So if, for example, you have Mars in Leo in the seventh, in order to have the principle of assertion and action operating fully in you, you need to experience yourself as a dramatic, special sort of person, and you need one-to-one relationships as an arena in which to bring out your dramatic self-assertion. It does not mean that relationships are the only area in which your Mars will work. They are a sort of necessary gateway for introducing your Mars energy to the world. If you do not have them and/or you do not experience yourself as dramatic or special then your Mars will not work very well. Just having this configuration will not automatically make you star material and great at relationships. This point is often not well understood and so leads to a lot of confusion. The usual way of interpreting Mars in Leo and the seventh would be to say that the person acts in a dramatic and regal manner and puts a lot of energy into relationships. It is perhaps more accurate to say that the person is *associated* with those attributes in some way. This point needs to be borne in mind rather than developed at this stage and it will generally be more convenient to use ordinary language for interpretation. With this in mind, let us work through Chart A.

Date: *12 May 1924*   Time: *10.09 AM GMT*   Place: *Birmingham*

Latitude: *52 N 30*   Longitude: *1 W 55*

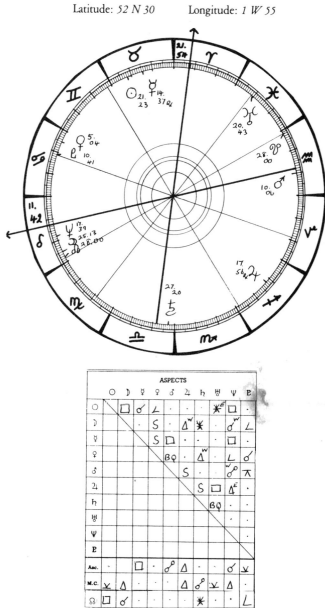

Figure 1.   Chart A.

ANALYSIS OF CHART A

(Chart A is that of Tony Hancock, one of the most successful and best-loved of English radio and television comedians. Data is from the Astrological Association and I have rectified the time from the given time of 10.00 a.m.)

☉ in ♉ and 10
To experience a central purpose for his life, the person needs stability, a sense of rootedness and solidity. He will probably manifest this as stubbornness, conservatism, self-indulgence, concern with money and material things. He will be drawn to circumstances of status, success, approval and recognition of his skills.

☉ □ ☽
Clash between central purpose and the means of expressing it. Powerful, discordant responses and behaviour. May be self-centred and over-sensitive. Deep-rooted habit patterns.

☉ ♂ ☿
Forceful, often dogmatic, speaking and thinking. Restless, highly strung, needs to be on the move. Perhaps poor awareness of other people's reactions to him.

☉ ∟ ♀
Strain between central purpose and affections. Warm but moody; can be sentimental. Prefers to compromise rather than really handle difficulties.

☉ * ♅
Possibility for developing new, original and exciting expressions of himself. Tends to be restless, impatient, always wanting to move on to something new. Liable to be hasty, over-excited.

☉ □ ♆
Sensitive, imaginative, impressionable. Sense of purpose is undermined by glamorous images of himself. Much self-deception, putting on an act for himself and others. Escapist, tends to avoid being clear about himself.

☉ ⊻ M
Mild tension between central purpose and conscious aims. Ambitious,

may be highly skilled and capable, but self-centred. Probably confident about what he can do but inclined to set unrealistic goals, to be perfectionist and discontented.

⊙ ☐ ⚇
Clash between central purpose and associations with others. Capacity for intense involvement with others but with possibility of snobbish, exclusive attitudes.

☽ in ♌ and 1
To experience a secure sense of identity, he needs to be a leader, the centre of attention, to behave in a dramatic manner. He will be drawn to circumstances of immediate self-assertion and self-expression.

☽ △ ♃
Security and expansion flow easily together. He will be sociable, outgoing, inclined to be extravagant in various ways. He tends to be too open to experience without enough discrimination.

☽ ✶ ♄
Security and restriction flow easily together. This is an aspect where limitations are easily put up with. Tendency to depression, withdrawal. Feelings seem frozen below a certain level and relationships are difficult. Liable to sense of inadequacy and inferiority.

☽ ☌ ♆
Defensive, tends to withdrawal, inclined to passivity and lethargy. Idealistic attitude to women. Powerful imagination, intuition.

☽ ∟ ♇
Very emotional and intense, rather fanatical sense of a mission in life. Over-control of feelings leading to much blocked energy, which may be self-destructive.

☽ △ M
Security needs and goals flow together easily. Aims in life are subject to moods and feelings but such moods and feelings can be harnessed to serve his goals. Tends to manoeuvre and manipulate rather than go for objectives openly.

☽ ☌ ⚇
Can be very clinging, demanding, nostalgic. Probably has a large circle

of friends on whom he depends for emotional support. May create upsets by making heavier demands than they can cope with.

☿ in ♄ and 10
Reasoning and communicating needs experience of stability to function and he will be drawn to circumstances of status, recognition and public success. There will be some rigidity and obstinacy of thinking yet with an air of substance and knowing what he is talking about. He will tend to be basically conventional in his thinking.

☿ □ ♂
Can be blunt, unsentimental, tactless, forceful in speech and thought. Irritable, witty, very restless. Enterprising but with a tendency to upset others.

☿ □ ♆
Powerful intuition and imagination but tends to be very confused in the expression of it. Many worries and vague fears, especially in situations that are novel or unstructured.

☿ □ A
Talks a lot, uses words to conceal feelings. Critical, complaining. Does not like to be committed to anything, nervous, restless, indecisive. Inclined to be amoral, to take the view that actions are justified if they work.

♀ in ♋ and 11
Needs the experience of emotional security, human relationships and nurturing for affections and values to function. This will probably manifest as intense loyalty and dependence in love relationships with considerable insecurity, jealousy and possessiveness. He needs considerable involvement with groups, a wide circle of friends and will be drawn to those circumstances.

♀ △ ♄
Tends to be cautious and defensive in relationships, may dislike being touched. Finds it difficult to accept compliments or other show of approval or affection.

♀ ∟ ♆
Rather stressful, idealistic need for love and affection. Very unrealistic about his personal affairs and relationships. May attract people who

behave badly and unreasonably or be that way himself.

♀ ♂ ♇

Very powerful sex drive, probably with considerable personal
magnetism. Energy may be so strong that it is largely blocked, with
corresponding frustrations and possibility of violence.

♂ in ♒ and 6

To assert himself effectively, he needs the experience of freedom, the
challenge to move into new fields, the opportunity to experiment.
This will probably manifest as excessive independence, discontent with
existing situations, stubborn, fixed ideas. He will be drawn to circumstances that involve techniques, routine work and possibly health.

♂ ☍ ♆

At best, can act in a truly inspired and inspiring way, but much
difficulty in knowing what he really wants. Tendency to lethargy,
passivity, general inability to muster and focus energy. Tendency to
escapism, maybe drink, drugs.

♂ ⊼ ♇

Very ambitious but one-sided, able to succeed by thrusting forward
without considering others. Uncompromising, wants to dominate and
to be in control.

♂ ☍ A

Presents himself in a heavy, intense manner. May not be overtly
aggressive but nevertheless creates many disputes and disagreements
in personal affairs. Tries to do everything by willpower and gets
exhausted. May be underlying, panicky fear.

♃ in ♐ and 5

To expand and grow psychologically and socially, needs a sense of
opportunities, wide horizons, freedom to move within a definite
structure. This will probably manifest as optimism, enthusiasm,
ambition. Drawn to circumstances in which he can experience being
in the limelight, using personal creativity.

♃ □ ♅

A quick grasp of situations, need for growth through inner
development. Independent. Very intuitive but may be too dogmatic
about and insistent on his intuitions in the face of opposition.

♃ △ ♆

Compassionate but unrealistic. Considerable difficulties in appreciating the difference between vision and reality. With the trine here, he may not even see that there is a problem. Very imaginative and impressionable. He may feel misunderstood and his efforts may frequently be misdirected.

♃ △ A

Open and expansive, jovial, takes an interest in other people and readily finds common ground with them. Generous with time and energy.

♃ △ M

Easy, confident, optimistic attitudes. Considerable emphasis on personal success with desire for fame and glory.

♄ in ♎ and 4

Sense of limitation activated by the experiences of personal relationships, balance and harmony. He will experience himself as being deficient in these areas or find them in some way disappointing. There will be a lack of spontaneity, a certain formality and distance in social relationships. He will be drawn to circumstances in which his sense of personal image is undermined and his immediate environment seems demanding and unloving.

♄ ☍ M

Hesitant, reserved, sense of inadequacy, probably not very self-aware. Feels misunderstood and frustrated. Very high standards for himself so rarely feels that what he has done is good enough.

♄ ✳ ☋

Cautious, reserved, liable to feel inadequate in groups. Expects total loyalty from associates or subordinates and can be dogmatic and inflexible with them.

♅ in 8

Insight, leaps of understanding, dependent on intense interaction with others. This will probably manifest as sudden attractions and sudden disenchantments, eccentric and unreliable behaviour. There may be some sexual difficulties.

♅ ⊻ M

Energetic, self-centred, willing to take risks. Independent, does not like working for others.

Ψ in 1

Presents himself to others with a lot of charisma and 'image'. People are drawn to the image but do not see the real person beneath it. His interactions with others are therefore not really satisfying.

Ψ ♂ A

As above. Vague and elusive, can be easily influenced. Intuitive understanding of other people's feelings.

Ψ Δ M

Tends to feel insecure and confused about his place in life. Finds it difficult to muster energy for personal goals unless they grip his imagination and seem to serve a larger purpose. If they do, he can create a powerful public image and may identify with it strongly.

♇ in 11

Group activities and relationships with friends are characterized by a need to dominate and control. There may be ruthlessness, egocentric behaviour, resulting in many upsets and crises.

♇ ⊻ A

Feels he has a lot of energy to be expressed, a message to be delivered. May be rigid, dogmatic, opinionated, with a strong need to be right. Thrusting attitude motivated by the desire to dominate and have power.

♇ ∟ ☊

Charisma, inspiring leadership, can motivate people to get things done. Desire to dominate, ruthlessness.

MC ♈

Sees himself and his goals as an individualist. There is a sense of 'me first', probably with the feeling that he is reaching too far ahead of others to get the support he wants to reach his objectives. Impatient, hasty, cannot be bothered with details. Inclined to rush ahead without proper groundwork.

Asc ♌

Presents himself in a dramatic, imposing, impressive way. Tends to seek the limelight and draw attention to himself. Comes on as very self-assured and dignified but rather cool under the bonhomie. Has considerable amount of presence.

In accordance with the usual practice, I have not interpreted the outer planets by sign. The house position of Uranus and Pluto is doubtful but, for the present purpose, I have taken them as being definitely eighth and eleventh, respectively. If the Node is taken as meaning associations with others, aspects to it definitely seem to work and I have used them. I am not so sure about sign and house positions, which I have omitted.

These notes are about the right length for the purpose of discovering the basic life themes in them. They could be made somewhat shorter by simply jotting down the appropriate keywords. Making them longer would tend to be too time-consuming and pointless in any case, since we are aiming to boil them down to half a dozen or so succinctly stated themes.

Up to this point, the analysis has been largely mechanical. I recommend doing it from first principles because this is an excellent exercise for fixing the principles of interpretation in the mind but you can use your favourite set of delineations if you prefer to. The second stage is not really much more difficult but it depends on cultivating the ability to see a pattern. There is no special psychic sense involved; it is the same as learning to see the essence of an argument or the plot of a novel.

All we have to do is go through the notes and pick out certain words that strike the eye because of the frequency with which they occur. Then we look for other attributes that can be associated with them until we can build up a statement that expresses a part of the person's character.

Usually, one or two of these themes will present themselves in the act of making the notes. In the case of this chart, we can hardly avoid seeing three themes which can be grouped as: 1. imaginative — impressionable — inspired; 2. cautious — defensive — inadequate; 3. ambitious — egocentric — controlling. There are others, but let us take these three to start with.

Having noticed a theme of impressionability, we can look through the notes again with this theme in mind to see if there is anything else that would link up with this characteristic.

We can see that the person is emotional, nostalgic, dependent on others and self-dramatizing. These are factors which would be likely to come into play along with the impressionability. We can put all this together in a brief statement.

1. Emotional and dependent, with much need for nurturing and support from others. Sensitivity and imagination will aggravate

this and he will draw a lot of attention to himself in rather dramatic ways to ensure he gets the support he needs.

Now we see what else would probably go with the cautious and defensive theme. Well, he is conventional, stubborn, self-indulgent and feels he is being got at. He is not very good at expressing feelings. So theme 2 might read:

2. The expression of feelings is inhibited and he is liable to a sense of being inadequate and inferior. He will want to cling to what he knows in order to protect this and he will be stubborn, concerned with money and possessions in some way, and generally cautious.

It could, of course, be argued that the conservatism could as well go along with the emotional dependence of theme 1. This is a good point at which to remind ourselves that what we are doing is producing information in a form that the client can recognize and react to — and ultimately benefit from. There is no one 'right' way to do it. We are engaged in the essentially arbitrary act of imposing a temporary order on the flux and chaos of the client's personality so that he can stop and take a look at it. To hark back to Chapter 1 for a moment, let us remind ourselves that we are dealing with the whole system of astrologer/chart/client. Laying the chart out in this way starts to have a very cut and dried look about it which we need to stay aware of and not accept at face value.

Theme 3 is 'ambitious — egocentric — controlling'. Other attributes cognate with this are forceful and dogmatic, low sensitivity to others' reactions, need for recognition and success, enterprising but tactless, ruthless, independent. These can be put together in some such statement as:

3. He will be ambitious and has the ability to succeed but there is a ruthless quality to his ambition. He needs to be in control and will be inconsiderate of the effects of his actions on others.

These three statements cover quite a lot of ground but there are other themes that still need to be brought out. Between five and eight seems to be the optimum number to look for. Fewer than five will not bring out enough of the material. More than eight starts to create too much similarity between themes.

Restlessness and impatience are another obvious theme. They may be linked up with bluntness and concern with innovation and techniques.

4.   He will be restless, impatient, hasty, often blunt or sarcastic. He will take work very seriously, perhaps to the point of obsession, and will be constantly seeking to improve his performance. There will be much anxiety, which will add to the impatience. Does not like to be too committed to anything.

We have not yet said anything about love and sex.

5.   Sexual feelings are powerful but rather severely blocked. His attitudes to women are unrealistic and so invite disappointment. He needs a lot of affection and nurturing but it is difficult for him to acknowledge that and to accept affection when it is given.

Escapism is another theme that needs to be developed:

6.   Tensions and worries frequently exhaust him and he will seek refuge in fits of lethargy and in various forms of escapism. Alcohol and drugs are an obvious danger here.

Finally, we can note the sociable, outgoing side of him:

7.   Sociable, outgoing, can be an extremely magnetic personality, generous and extravagant, with the ability to attract large numbers of friends. There will be a tendency for there to be something unrealistic in this and he may attract more than his share of people who behave badly, or be that way himself.

We are now in a good position to do a session with this client. We have seven major themes of his life, stated in such a way that they make useful starting-points for discussion. In addition, we have the full notes, which can be referred to for detail or to distinguish between various levels of the personality. For example, it may be useful, from time to time, to be able to specify that certain attributes are related to certain planets. We might, for example, want to draw his attention to the fact that the Leo function has a very automatic and defensive quality with the Moon there, yet at the same time also a learned and acquired quality, with it being the Ascendant sign.

I have not interpreted signs on house cusps, partly because that starts to make the notes unwieldy, partly because that is the basis of another method of information display which we shall be dealing with in Chapter 5. However, with the chart to hand, if the discussion centres on, for example, work, we can see that with Capricorn on the sixth house, his attitudes to work will be those of being status conscious, industrious and so on.

We are not so much concerned with extracting the last possible drop of information as with assembling most of it in a useable way. Students often think that they have to note every nuance of every factor but that is impossible. The art of astrology consists at least as much in knowing what pieces of information are appropriate as in having a wide knowledge of interpretational meanings, important though that obviously is.

This layout of half a dozen or so major themes, backed by more detailed notes, is best used in a face-to-face counselling session, where there is room for plenty of discussion and client participation. Clearly it is not quite so suitable for written work. Other layouts more suitable for written, or tape recorded, work will be given later. Although the trick of picking out the themes of the chart is easy enough once it has been learned, it needs to be cultivated and practised. In the next chapter, therefore, we will continue to illustrate it, using another chart.

3.
DISCOVERING CHART THEMES (2)

ANALYSIS OF CHART B

(Chart B is that of the poet, W. H. Auden. He was one of the first writers to make extensive use of such modern images as pylons and aircraft in his verse and, initially at least, his writing was motivated by a good deal of political commitment.)

☉ in ♓ and 4
To experience a central purpose for his life, the person needs to link with a sense of greater purpose and to feel himself to be part of a greater whole. He will probably manifest this as idealism, sensitivity, imagination, perhaps gullibility and passivity/escapism. He will be much concerned with creating emotional stability through family or other circles of people and with his own self-image and sense of belonging.

☉ ⌐ ♀
Affectionate, outgoing, strong emotional and sexual nature. Tends to compromise at a surface level rather than handle difficulties in relationships and may be more concerned with his own needs than with other people's reactions, which may lead to some disappointment in love.

☉ □ ♂
Assertive, aggressive, courageous and enterprising. He will be likely to make an issue in some way of the ability to act effectively. Strong physical sexuality, perhaps rather undiscriminating.

☉ △ ♃
Optimistic, generous. A strong desire for recognition and a capacity

Date: *21 February 1907*   Time: *11.00 PM*   Place: *York*

Latitude: *53 N 58*   Longitude: *1 W 07*

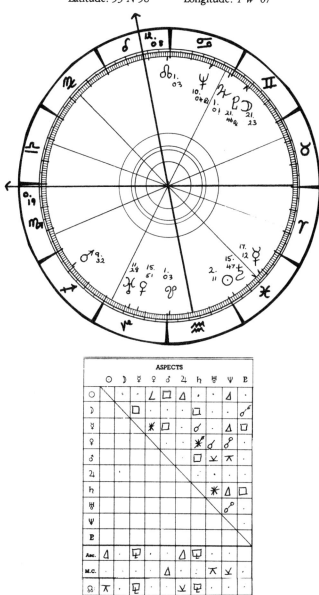

Figure 2.   Chart B.

for enjoying life. Can be extravagant, ostentatious, self-centred and superior, concerned always with his own advantage.

☉ △ ♆

Sensitive, imaginative, impressionable. Inclined to think in generalities rather than particulars, which can be a form of escapism and avoiding clarity. Liable to self-deception, always able to put on an act.

☉ △ A

Confident, individualistic demeanour. Presents himself in a forceful way, often overwhelming, though perhaps charmingly so. Great need to be recognized and looked up to by others.

☉ ⊼ ☋

Capacity for intense social life. Able to co-operate readily with others but with some degree of strain. There may be snobbish, exclusive attitudes and the feeling that people are mostly not good enough.

☽ in ♓ and 8

To experience a secure sense of identity, he needs to be involved in many experiences and have a sense of being well-informed. He will probably manifest this as flexibility, curiosity and gregariousness. He will be drawn to circumstances involving joint goals, use of energy and of hidden knowledge and probing to the roots of things.

☽ □ ☿

Strong tendency to verbalize, to be mentally active as much to conceal, control or avoid feelings as to express them. Often witty, quick to grasp the essence of an argument. Self-doubting and self-critical.

☽ □ ♄

Cautious and careful in expressing feelings. Tends to be private and withdrawn, feelings seem frozen below a certain level. Inclined to set habits, prefers order, structure and routine in his life. May have sense of inadequacy and inferiority.

☽ ☌ ♇

Highly emotional and intense but with great need to control it so much energy will be blocked. Strong sense of purpose in his life. Tends to distrust spontaneity, the free flow of feelings.

☿ in ♓ and 5

Reasoning and communicating needs faith and a sense of greater purpose in order to function and will be characterized by imagination, intuition, idealism. He will be drawn to circumstances of creativity and personal self-expression. He will probably be able to express himself verbally in a very idiosyncratic manner.

☿ ✱ ♀

Agreeable and charming, may be easily embarrassed and may take the view that personal matters should be kept hidden. A natural ability for verbal self-expression, perhaps tending to be rather facile.

☿ □ ♂

Can be blunt, unsentimental, tactless, impatient, careless of other people's feelings. Somewhat unreliable because easily deflected from a stated course. Irritable, witty, extremely restless. Enterprising but with the tendency to upset others.

☿ ♂ ♄

Pride in being clear and realistic but liable to confuse realism with pessimism. Good powers of concentration but can be too narrow and rigid in outlook. Able to think profoundly, to confront difficult issues. Industrious, conscientious. Good organizing ability.

☿ △ ♆

Powerful intuition, imagination but expression of ideas may be obscure or too general. Also may be difficult to follow because he tends to take too much of the listener's knowledge for granted. Tendency to worries and vague fears.

☿ □ ♇

Speech and thought very intense, strongly directed and purposeful. May be very opinionated, with a dislike of learning from others and a preference for teaching himself. Can be ruthlessly critical, so obsessed with making a point that what the other person says is not heard or valued.

☿ ⊔ A

Inclined to be very talkative, may use a lot of words as a smoke screen for his feelings. Critical, complaining, skilled at 'selling himself'. Inclined to be amoral, to take the view that something is acceptable if it works or if one can get away with it.

☿ ⊡ ☊
Tends to want the support of others before expressing his own views.
He will be inclined to stick to some kind of party line but be skilled
at turning it to his own advantage.

♀ in ♑ and 8
For affections and sense of values to function, he needs the experience
of social recognition based on his personal achievements. This will
tend to manifest as ambition, resourcefulness and responsibility, with
perhaps an authoritarian attitude and too ruthless a sense of personal
advantage. He will be drawn to circumstances which involve
communicating, expressing ideas and developing concrete knowledge.

♀ * ♄
Tends to be cautious and defensive in relationships, to feel inadequate
or rejected. Inhibition of creative impulses, perhaps avoidance of or
renunciation of parenthood. Tends to disapprove of himself and others,
may find it difficult to accept compliments or other show of approval
or affection.

♀ ☌ ♅
Can be very excitable, wanting drama and sensation in relationships
but also subject to sudden turn-offs. May be casual, informal,
promiscuous. May be much blocking of sexual energy because it needs
a different expression than is socially acceptable.

♀ ☍ ♆
Idealizes need for love and affection, perhaps because of childhood
lack. May be unrealistic about personal affairs and relationships.
Impressionable, enjoys mystery, strong tendency to believe what he
wants to believe. May have guilt feelings about sex. Possibly tends
to attract people who behave badly or unreasonably.

♂ in ♐ and 2
In order to act effectively, he needs a sense of wide horizons and
possibilities, a desire to discover a broader viewpoint. This will probably
manifest as qualities of being expansive, philosophical and persuasive.
He will be drawn to circumstances which involve gaining and using
resources and talents. Action will tend to have the goals of self-esteem,
increase in material value.

♂ □ ♄

Can use his energy in very precise, disciplined, controlled ways. Tends to be harsh and demanding of himself and others. May be severe sexual repressions with the frustrated energy turning to coldness or cruelty. May cling to bitter feelings about the past.

♂ ⊻ ♅

May be compulsive over-achiever, courageous and original. Quick, nervous, jumpy disposition and body movements. Can be self-willed and obstinate, yet with tendency to act hastily and prematurely.

♂ ⊼ ♆

Vivid imagination, practical use of intangible energies. Can act in a truly inspired and inspiring way. Negatively, this may become manipulation. May find it difficult to know what he really wants, with some inclination to lethargy and passivity.

♂ Δ M

Seeks to impress others and create opportunities for himself by emphasizing his own individuality. Distrusts authority. Likes to see self as tough, realistic and uncompromising. Usually can take the initiative effectively.

♃ in ♋ and 8

To expand and grow psychologically and socially, he needs emotional security, warm human relationships and privacy of feelings. This will probably manifest as an emphasis on protective (including self-protective) and nurturing behaviour. He will be drawn to circumstances involving joint goals and use of energies and resources and involving hidden knowledge and probing to the roots of things.

♃ Δ A

Open, expansive, takes an interest in other people. May seem casual and dismissive of things most people regard as serious. Generous with his time and energy.

♃ ⊻ ☋

Willing to put much energy into relationships but generally motivated by the desire to gain advantage for himself. This can be cynical manipulation but, positively, it can be a genuine contribution to others out of enlightened self-interest.

♄ in ♓ and 4

His sense of limitation is activated by the experience of, or the desire for, wholeness and a greater or transcendent purpose. He will experience himself as being deficient in these areas or find they are disappointing in some way. He will feel his imagination or intuition to be limited and will be drawn to circumstances that undermine his self-image and where the immediate environment seems demanding and unloving.

♄ ✳ ♅

Considerable inner stress and tension, striving to break out of set patterns and yet wanting to maintain them. Sudden swings in moods and sudden failures of energy. May have a disrupting effect on authority and existing institutions.

♄ △ ♆

Confusion, sense of having no 'backbone'. Tendency to passivity, resignation, feeling undermined. Against this, there is likely to be a great striving for clarity, refusal to accept unnecessary obscurity.

♄ □ ♇

Can drive himself very hard but with tendency to create situations in which others block success, through opposition or indifference. Dislikes revealing himself or probing his own motives.

♄ ⊼ A

Hesitant, reserved, feelings of inadequacy. Responsible, has a strong sense of propriety to the point of being rigid. Inclined to pessimistic attitudes.

♄ ⊼ ☋

Tends to be cautious and reserved in groups but will take any responsibilities seriously once they have been incurred. Expects total loyalty from associates or subordinates.

♅ in 3

Insight and leaps of understanding depend on the plentiful exchange of information and ideas with others. This will probably manifest as originality of expression and the ability to create new ways of saying things.

♅ ☍ ♆

Tends to be impractical, absent-minded, other-worldly. Powerful idealism, but poor grasp of reality and can be fanatical in pursuit of ideals.

♅ ⊼ **M**

Energetic, somewhat self-centred. Willing to take risks. Creative use of imagination and intuition. Independent, does not like working for others. Liable to many changes of interests and purpose. Dislikes routine and can often succeed through sudden, intuitive actions.

♆ in 9

In matters to do with a philosophy of life, higher forms of education and broad principles, he has a lot of charisma and 'image', though he is also probably subject to much confusion about these matters himself.

♆ ⊻ **M**

Tends to feel confused and insecure about his place in life. He may have difficulty in mustering energy for personal goals unless he can create a convincing public image to operate from.

♇ in 8

Joint goals and use of energies — including sexuality — are characterized by a need to dominate and control. There may be a good deal of ruthlessness and egocentric behaviour in these areas. He may feel that he needs to surrender control to others but be afraid of doing so.

MC ♌

Sees himself and his goals from the standpoint of being a natural leader. He needs a lot of praise and response from others in order to function well in terms of career and will be inclined to be rather demanding and dramatic to ensure that he obtains this.

Asc ♏

Presents himself to the world as a rather intense, secretive person, with much inner power but difficult to get to know. At the same time, will appear much concerned with relationships and will probably give them a very high value in his life.

Again, we will go through the material and organize it into about half a dozen themes. One theme that, for me at least, stands out is the emphasis on communicating. Here is a person who needs a lot of interaction with others, he needs to spread his own ideas around and he needs to be open to the ideas of others. He will have original ways of doing this and be inclined to have strong opinions. So we might express theme 1. as:

1. A big emphasis on communicating and learning, needing to know what is going on in the world. Gregarious and talkative, with original and innovative ways of expressing himself. He can inspire other people through his own gift of words and may, to some extent, see himself as a leader or teacher.

Linked to this to some extent is the need to create emotional stability and a sense of belonging. This need is connected with a desire for recognition and success.

2. A deep concern with creating emotional stability and support. He will largely try to gain this through his personal achievements. He may feel that he can only gain love by first gaining the respect of others for what he can do.

There is a certain emotional coldness and reserve.

3. Idealistic need for love but with much coldness and repression. He can be distant and aloof, rather impersonal. His attitude to relationships may be unusual in some way (he was, in fact, homosexual) but relationships will nevertheless be very important to him.

The coldness covers up a deep intensity and vulnerability.

4. Very emotional, intense and sensitive. He cannot ignore this but he does not like to explore it and may feel it a duty to conceal his difficulties from others. He is generally well able to do this, partly from a considerable capacity for enjoying life as it comes along, together with the ability to project a powerful air of confidence.

There is a lot of idealism and the need to see himself as part of a larger whole and a seeking for understanding as well as concrete knowledge.

5. He has a strong sense of purpose in his life and he will need
    to discover what it is by dedicating himself to some larger purpose.
    Philosophy and religion are likely to be of major importance to
    him.

Finally, we need to say something about his sexual attitudes.

6. An assertive, even aggressive, sexual nature, not particularly
    refined and inclined to be somewhat freewheeling. Probably
    makes a clear distinction between sex and love and, in sexual
    matters, he may be enthusiastic but impersonal.

I would suggest as an exercise, that you go through the notes both
for this chart and chart A and organize them into themes for yourself.
The ones you come up with should bear a strong resemblance to the
ones I have suggested but you might well wish to emphasize slightly
different elements in the notes and to put them together in different
ways. Better still, write your own notes and extract the themes from
those. You should draw out the same basic patterns but seen from
your own angle. It cannot be said or emphasized too often that astrology
only works in terms of the complete system of astrologer/chart/client.
As I have said in Chapter 1, astrological factors have a wide spectrum
of meanings. The ones I am using in this book represent that part
of the spectrum which best suits my own astrologer/chart/client system.
Other astrologers will be happier with a different part of the spectrum.
Indeed, much of the art of interpretation lies in discovering the right
part of the spectrum of meanings for your particular temperament
and approach. An astrological chart is not some kind of objective
personality test which can be switched on to provide an automatic
standard read-out, as if it were measuring blood sugar. It sometimes
looks that way (and some writers encourage us to suppose that it *is*
that way) but every interpretation/synthesis is, or should be, a unique
event and a fresh stretching of your understanding of the meanings
of the chart factors.

Again, to repeat a point made in Chapter 1, there is no reason why
you should not use standard delineations for the notes in using this
method of themes, *provided* you understand the basic principles of
how the delineations are arrived at. I would, in fact, recommend doing
that since it saves time. But ideally the delineations should be the
ones that you have arrived at for yourself. Probably every astrologer
needs to create his own personal interpretation manual made up of
the meanings which he has found to work and whose derivation he

thoroughly understands. It takes several years of involvement in astrology to be able to do this and, in the meantime, other people's texts are a good substitute.

In the next chapter we shall develop the idea of themes by considering a psychological tool known as 'subpersonality theory'. This will give us a deeper understanding of the way in which the chart themes work and how they interact with each other.

4.
SUBPERSONALITIES AND CHART THEMES

You will have noticed that some of the themes that emerge from the two charts we have analysed in Chapters 2 and 3 contradict each other while others are rather similar.

In Chart A, theme 1 is to do with being very dependent on others. It suggests a personality that is rather immature and demanding. In contrast, theme 3, which is ambitious, controlling and very tough, is so different that it is almost like another personality. Again, theme 7, the sociable, magnetic and charming one, is completely different from the other two. We would get very different impressions of the subject of the chart depending on which of the themes were uppermost at the time we met him.

Theme 6 — escapism — seems a kind of natural ally of theme 1 and so is theme 5 — sexual inhibition. Theme 4, the anxiety and restlessness, more or less lines up with theme 3. Theme 2, the stubbornness, could go with either one side or the other. It is as though there were about seven different personalities, some of whom would get along well together and some of whom would disagree violently.

It is, in fact, useful to consider these different facets of the individual as being distinct 'subpersonalities' and there is a branch of psychological theory which has made an extensive study of them. This work has mainly been done by the followers of Assagioli's Psychosynthesis school. In this chapter we shall take a brief look at these ideas. The reader who is interested mainly in the practicalities of organizing the chart material can skip this chapter at a first reading since an understanding of subpersonalities is concerned not so much with chart synthesis as with helping someone become a better astrologer (like the grasp of the basic questions about the nature of astrology that we discussed in Chapter 1).

There is nothing particularly difficult or esoteric about the idea of subpersonalities. We shift between several subpersonalities during the course of a day, or even an hour. For example, think of a day when, perhaps, you are going to a party that you are looking forward to in the evening, but meanwhile have to finish a job at work. Working hard under pressure, you concentrate on the job in hand and have little time for being sociable. If someone makes a joke or a remark that in other circumstances would have amused you, you dismiss it with a grunt or ignore it. You are operating in a subpersonality that is characterized by the qualities of being serious and purposeful, perhaps humourless and harrassed. If you think about the coming party at all, it is difficult to imagine it or to feel enthusiastic about it. It seems to belong to an entirely different world and so it does. This hardworking subpersonality has a world-view of its own and its own particular wants and needs.

When the job is finished, you take a train home. It has been a hard day; you feel tired and withdrawn. All you want to do is huddle into a corner and hide behind your newspaper. Not only does the idea of the party seem remote but so does the purpose and energy that were so evident when you were working. Now, a different subpersonality has taken over, one that is quiet and withdrawn, perhaps helpless and demanding, which wants to be looked after and made a fuss of.

A bath and a meal take care of this subpersonality's needs and you reach the party in fairly good shape. Once there, and with the aid of a couple of drinks, you become warm and expansive, in the mood to laugh and enjoy yourself. Now, you are operating in a fun-loving subpersonality which, again, has its own wants and needs and worldview. Both the harrassed and withdrawn subpersonalities now seem remote and alien. Ordinarily, we would just say that we were in different moods at the different times and not pay very much attention to the phenomenon.

As with any other psychological theory, the question is not so much whether subpersonalities exist as whether it is useful to suppose that they do. Is the idea of a crowd of separate subpersonalities, interacting and quarrelling with each other, a workable one for understanding human nature and, in our case, for better understanding how to apply the information which is available from an astrological chart?

If we do adopt the idea of subpersonalities, we can use it to pin down and explore feelings and behaviour in ourselves and our clients which may seem no more than trifling moods and yet which may contain keys to a very large range of our actions and attitudes to the world. Furthermore, as we have already seen from the Tony Hancock chart (p.28), we can get a fair idea of some of the major subpersonalities from the chart alone. I stress *a fair idea* as it is evident from our examination of the two charts that there is a certain arbitrary quality to the way the themes are put together. Working at a desk on the chart is a very different matter from working with an actual client. The subpersonalities that are present in the client may or may not correspond exactly with the chart themes that we have extracted. Most likely they will not. But they will be near enough, as a first approximation, to shed light on the subpersonalities and assist the client to become more conscious of them.

Usually, in working with subpersonalities, it helps to give them names so as to get a more definite picture of them. *Bearing in mind that, at this stage, the chart is only giving us a first approximation*, let us tentatively do this for the chart themes for Tony Hancock.

Theme 1 — emotional and dependent — we might call Demanding Child. Theme 2 — the stubborn one — could be The Bulldog. Theme 3 is The Winner or, perhaps, The Boss. Theme 4 could be The Perfectionist. Theme 5 might be The Romantic or, perhaps, The Puritan. Theme 6 is really another childlike one and could perhaps be called Withdrawn Child. Theme 7 can be called The Extravert or The Life and Soul of the Party.

These names are not necessarily the ones that the person himself would choose. Obviously, there will be all kinds of nuances that he will be aware of and that we, as the astrologer, cannot be. Theme 2, for example, has a good deal of feelings of inferiority about it and the person himself may see it rather as a Victim than a Bulldog. The themes or subpersonalities that we arrive at on paper are no more than a useful rough blocking out of the territory. They need to be defined more accurately by discussion with the client and in no circumstances should they be imposed upon the client.

The point of identifying a subpersonality is that once we are conscious of it we can start to exercise some control over it. This is achieved by *dis*identifying from it. It is as though consciousness consists of a crowd of subpersonalities, all with passionate feelings and/or powerful points of view, who are constantly trying to grab the centre of the stage. Floating among them is a sense of 'I', a point of pure consciousness and will, which is usually experienced only fleetingly because it is most often trapped in one or other of the subpersonalities. In the hypothetical example I suggested earlier (of being hard-pressed at work and going to a party in the evening) I was supposing, as would usually be the case, that the person was totally identified with the subpersonality that had the executive position at the time. Just as enjoying yourself at a party is nearly inconceivable when you are under pressure at work, so the pressured, irritable creature in the work situation seems like a dream when you are relaxed and enjoying the evening.

Sometimes the sense of 'I' can be trapped by a powerful subpersonality and remain so for days at a time. Subpersonalities are very unwilling to give up their starring role! They usually have it taken from them by another subpersonality, as in the example, in a way that the person as a whole remains more or less unconscious of. Suppose, though, in the example, none of the other subpersonalities were strong enough to take away the executive role from the hardworking, harrassed one. In that case you would remain in a grim, preoccupied mood throughout the train journey *and* the party.

It might seem that a particular annoyance or problem at work was causing the persistence of the mood. In effect, this would be the subpersonality justifying holding on to the executive position. Once you are aware that it *is* a subpersonality, you can begin to break its hold consciously, instead of having to wait for another subpersonality to elbow it out of the limelight.

Often we have subpersonalities that we do not even know about, though other people react to them and we wonder, perhaps indignantly, why they should react in such a way. Such subpersonalities hardly ever reach the centre of the stage but they make their presence felt, nevertheless. The sort of general feeling of who we are that we usually mean when we talk or think about 'myself' is not the disidentified sense of 'I'. Rather it is a group of subpersonalities that are best adapted to dealing with the world. There will, typically, be a Nice Guy, a Good Neighbour, Responsible Citizen, Loving Parent, Considerate Husband/Wife.

There are also some disreputable ones that we know are there but which we prefer to keep in the wings as much as possible. There might be a lazy one, a selfish one, a greedy one, one with a violent temper, and so on. If one of these does take centre stage for any length of time, it seems completely alien to us afterwards and we are likely to say 'I was beside myself', or 'I don't know what came over me'. It is as though the respectable subpersonalities are grouped together as members of an exclusive club. They have to recognize, however reluctantly, the existence of the others and have dealings with them but they will never allow them to join the club. In terms of the way we normally see it, we *are* the reasonable, acceptable subpersonalities and we have a few unfortunate human failings as well.

Then there is a third group of subpersonalities that are only likely to come to consciousness, if they ever do, in unusual circumstances or under psychological treatment or analysis. Some of these deeply hidden subpersonalities would be judged as evil by the central club, others would be thought to be impossibly heroic and noble.

In fact, no subpersonality is ultimately evil, however vicious and degraded its manifestations might be. The Psychosynthesis view of the psyche is that it consists of an ultimate Self, or Higher Self, which operates first through a region known as the Superconscious, or Higher Unconscious. Put very simply, the Superconscious contains, in an abstract way, the qualities that make up human life. A few of them are Power, Creativity, Courage, Love, Patience, Understanding, Wisdom, Joy. When our ordinary consciousness makes contact with the Superconscious, the result is experiences of ecstasy, inspiration, light, beauty.

The next region is ordinary consciousness. This is really another field of unconsciousness with a kind of spotlight of consciousness sweeping about it, illuminating its various contents. The spotlight of consciousness contains the sense of 'I' though this, as we have seen, is mostly trapped in the various subpersonalities, mainly those who make up the 'respectable' central club.

Below this region is the Lower Unconscious, which is more or less the Freudian unconscious, containing childhood traumas and forgotten material. A major, indeed vital, difference between the Freudian view and the Psychosynthesis view is that Freud sees the psyche developing upwards from the unconscious, which is mostly negative, where the Psychosynthesis view is that the psyche manifests downwards from the Higher Self, which is entirely positive and, moreover, positive in a way which we cannot even begin to grasp at the ordinary level of consciousness.

So all subpersonalities are manifestations, ultimately, of the Higher Self. Specifically, they are distortions, at the level of ordinary consciousness and of the Lower Unconscious, of the abstract qualities that the Higher Self emanates.

There are virtually an infinite number of qualities and so virtually an infinite number of subpersonalities. There is probably a sub-personality for every single factor in the chart — every sign and house position and house cusp and ruler, every aspect, every midpoint configuration and so on. Many of them, of course, are so similar as to be indistinguishable for all practical purposes, which is why a broad grouping into about half a dozen major themes reduces the problem to manageable proportions.

Some subpersonalities have a kind of collective quality and are present in everybody. Others are unique to the individual person.

Everybody has some kind of a tough, practical subpersonality, a gentle, idealistic one and, in Western cultures at any rate, a subpersonality that is essentially an emotionally deprived or rejected child. Even the collective subpersonalities, however, will have different attributes in different people. The rejected child, for example, may be hurt, sulky, angry, vindictive, anxious to please, etc. according to other factors.

Each subpersonality is, as its name implies, a personality in miniature. It has a set of gestures, expressions, body postures, attitudes, needs, wants and an individual view of the world. Sometimes the difference between two subpersonalities is so marked that it literally seems as though we are dealing with two different people. In ordinary life we may not often notice marked transitions from one to another. We certainly recognize shifts in emphasis over periods of a few hours. For example, the question of what sort of mood a colleague is in crops up frequently in most jobs. Some days he may be all joviality (the Benevolent Uncle subpersonality) and other days he is more like a bear with a sore head (the Scrooge subpersonality).

In a counselling session, where we are probing for subpersonalities, we often see sudden shifts from one to another. One good example is a woman whose chart was mostly Taurus, Gemini and Leo, with Scorpio rising. Throughout most of the interview, she sat in a very upright and rigid posture, with a set and determined expression on her face, speaking in a rather clipped and matter-of-fact way. There was a much softer side to her, which was shown in the chart by Mars in Pisces and Venus in Cancer square to Neptune. The two sub-personalities could be called Career Woman and Romantic Belle.

This client's sense of 'I' was mostly stuck in Career Woman and this subpersonality did its best to keep the executive position throughout the entire interview. She recognized the existence of Romantic Belle but despised her and tried to keep her down. Nevertheless, every time I mentioned Romantic Belle, that sub-personality seized the opportunity to express itself. The client changed her posture dramatically, lounging gracefully in the armchair instead of sitting bolt upright on the edge of it. Her expression softened, she smiled more, her voice became lower and softer and she spoke a little more slowly. This would last for four or five minutes, then Career Woman would grab the reins again and my client would revert to her efficient, practical demeanour.

In broad terms, the two qualities that were being manifested by these two subpersonalities were Power by Career Woman and Love by Romantic Belle. In the overall economy of this person's psyche, Power very much had the upper hand. Love was being forced to express itself in a way that was rather artificial, clinging and over-seductive. Indeed, difficulties in relationships was one of the issues of the interview. The client needed to learn to accept both Career Woman and Romantic Belle, so that Romantic Belle could have a chance to grow and develop. Subpersonalities can mature and change but it is hard for them to do so if they are always being squashed by a more powerful subpersonality.

We need to develop a feel for and experience of subpersonalities rather than just see them as intellectual concepts. A good way to do this is to discover some of our own subpersonalities. Most of the standard exercises for eliciting subpersonalities involve visualizations. For those who find visualization difficult, there is a more direct method.

First, the visualization exercise. Choose a time when you will not be interrupted for half an hour or so. Take the phone off the hook if necessary and get comfortable. Take a few deep breaths and relax. Imagine yourself in a meadow. It is a warm, sunny day with a clear sky. Make it as real for yourself as you can. Hear the birds singing. Feel the soft breeze on your face and ruffling your clothes. Stamp your feet firmly on the grass. (In the imaginary scene, that is. You can do it with your real feet as well, if you are sitting up. It will help.) Bend down and feel a blade of grass between your finger and thumb.

When you feel established in the scene take a look around the meadow. See some trees in full leaf, maybe a fluffy white cloud or two in the sky. Note where the sun is. Then notice a path leading out of the meadow to a house. Walk along the path until you come to the door of the house. On the door is a sign saying SUBPERSONALITIES. All your subpersonalities are behind that door. Knock on the door and invite three of the subpersonalities to come out. Just accept whatever happens and don't try to impose preconceived ideas on it. The subpersonalities may be any age or either sex.

Watch and see how the subpersonalities relate to each other. Do they get on well together? Do they quarrel or ignore each other? After a while, focus on one subpersonality. See what you like and dislike about it. Then approach it and begin to talk to it. See what you have to say to each other. Ask the subpersonality what it wants and why. Then ask it what it needs and why.

Be flexible in your attitude to the subpersonalities and keep your sense of humour. If necessary, pester them until you get answers to your questions. One man discovered a subpersonality who took the form of a black uniformed SS officer, jackboots and all, who was very arrogant and cold and who refused, contemptuously, to say anything. Eventually, the man said, 'Ve haf vays off making you talk!' The subpersonality appreciated the ironic joke and began to relate.

Then *become* the subpersonality (this is doing consciously what you do unconsciously all the time) and ask yourself, 'What do I want? What do I need? What is my view of the world?' Become yourself again and take a look at the subpersonality. Then ask yourself what your life would be like if you were that subpersonality permanently.

Now do the same things with each of the other two subpersonalities in turn. Finally, get all three of them around you and have a ray of the sun envelop you all in warmth and light. See if any changes or developments take place in the subpersonalities. When you are ready, open your eyes and take a few moments to experience yourself being back in the room. Write a short account of what happened. Give the subpersonalities names, if you have not already done so and, finally, see what configurations in your astrological chart correspond to them.

This is a fairly elaborate exercise and takes a while to perform. The second, more direct, way of getting in touch with subpersonalities is by simply noticing your own patterns of behaviour. Then imagine a character in a play that had been created to show that behaviour pattern. What would it be like? What would your life be like if you *were* that subpersonality all the time? Do this with whatever patterns and feelings that come up, e.g. happiness, generosity, meanness, anger, clumsiness. Again, give the subpersonalities names, see how they are described in your chart, and see if you can discover what abstract quality they embody, bearing in mind that these are *always* positive. Meanness, for example, is not an abstract quality, or not in the sense of being a transpersonal quality. It might be a distortion of Order or Simplicity.

Obviously you do not have to be an expert in subpersonalities in order to do astrology, but an acquaintance with at least as much of the subject as we have looked at in this chapter will help you to see a chart in terms of its themes. Though I do not particularly recommend that subpersonality theory be used in the actual counselling session, it can at times be useful, especially when a client is having difficulty in seeing how his chart can have very contradictory themes.

Up to now, we have assumed that the chart analysis is a preliminary to a face-to-face dialogue. In many cases, of course, this is not so, and in the next chapter we will look at some formats more suited to written or tape recorded work.

5.
HOUSES IN SYNTHESIS

Using the basic themes of the chart is a technique best suited to a face-to-face dialogue, where the client is prepared to participate to a considerable extent. In my view, this is the most potentially fruitful use of astrology. However, not every client wants to do this and some have to be dealt with by mail order because they live too far away for a visit. In these circumstances, a written or tape recorded report is the only way of working. The astrologer will need some kind of format for displaying the information which enables him to keep control of it and yet is sufficiently flexible to allow him to deal at length with whatever issues may need to be dealt with.

One such format is to take the houses as being circumstances of life and to interpret the chart round the clock, showing what needs (the sign on the cusp) and drives (planets ruling the sign and in the house) are linked with these circumstances. This format enables us to write or dictate a discursive report that is nevertheless held within a developing framework.

Circumstances of life can be things that are already present (or at least easily available) or they can be things that are desired, or goals. The houses of the chart can thus be defined in either of these two ways. The signs on the cusps then show not only the kind of needs that will be invoked by a particular experience but the qualities which have to be developed in order to reach a certain goal. For example, Aries on the seventh house indicates that one-to-one relationships provoke a need to be assertive and competitive. Equally, it is an indication that if relationships are to be handled effectively, the qualities of assertion and aggressiveness will need to be developed.

Obviously, we must have a clear idea of what the houses mean. I find it more useful to talk in terms of psychological meanings but there is no reason why traditional, concrete meanings should not be used. Let us first look at the meanings of houses in psychological terms.

HOUSE MEANINGS

1. Being one's characteristic self, actualizing one's potential, presenting oneself to the world in a way that works.
2. Gaining and using personal resources, both material and psychological. Having an experience of self-worth and stability.
3. Using one's mind to make sense of immediate experiences. Gaining and using concrete knowledge so that one knows how to deal with life.
4. Creating a sense of identity in response to inner and outer pressures. Having a sense of belonging and so being supported by one's immediate environment.
5. The experience of self-expression as emotional release. Putting one's personal stamp on the environment; being physically, mentally and emotionally creative.
6. Curbing self-expression to allow for the needs of others. Learning techniques, routines for getting along. Self-analysis, learning from mistakes.
7. Recognizing that the needs of others are as valid as one's own. Finding self-fulfilment through the awareness and acceptance of relationship.
8. Deep involvement with something other than oneself. The experience of exchanging energy or resources with others, perhaps with sacrifice of personal will.
9. Extending one's horizons, learning the 'why' of life rather than the 'how'. Using the mind to make sense of broad social or emotional experiences.
10. Creating status and a public image through contributing to a larger whole. Being accepted within a social structure, having a sense of confidence and rightness within a group.
11. Reaping the rewards of contributing to the group. The experience of friendship, self-expression through group activities, with an attitude of equality to other group members.
12. Confronting one's physical, mental and emotional inadequacies. Learning to move on from limiting patterns and taking responsibility for one's life through commitment to one's inner resources.

These meanings do not replace the more concrete, traditional meanings. They include them and expand on them so as to make the use of houses more widely applicable to a range of problems. For example, the fourth house has the meaning of feeling supported by the environment and thus having a secure sense of personal identity. Issues around this may relate to a concrete home and family or they may not.

The meanings of the eleventh and twelfth houses are less easily grasped than the others. To some extent this is because they represent experiences which our ego-orientated culture devalues and teaches us to avoid. This is particularly so of the twelfth house, whose traditional meaning is almost entirely negative. The traditional meaning of the eleventh — friends, hopes and wishes — is rather feeble for a house which is directly related to the powerful fifth. At this point, few of us really know how to find self-fulfilment through total commitment to group activities.

We will now go through Chart A (see Fig. 1, p. 19) again and interpret it with the houses format.

ANALYSIS OF CHART A BY HOUSES

Whether we are doing a written report or a tape recording, it is a good idea to have a list of the house meanings on a duplicated sheet as a preface so that the client is prepared for the style of presentation.

This example report has been kept fairly sparse. The significators in parentheses are not intended for the client but to make the deductions clearer. In practice, we can use this format to address issues that concern the client at some length in the appropriate section or sections. For instance, there were severe marriage problems in this case. If this had been a real client and he had mentioned them to start with, the specific issues to do with these problems could have been discussed at greater length.

Since the report is something that has to stand on its own rather than be the subject for discussion, it is appropriate to address the client directly.

1. The way you present yourself to the world, actualizing your potential, just being your natural, characteristic self, brings out your need for the limelight. The most natural way for you to be is to stamp your personality on the environment, to be sunny and rather autocratic. You need to be the leader, not so much for what you can do, though that is important, but for who you are. You need much applause and feedback in this area of your life, which is, obviously, a most basic one. There is quite a lot of insecurity here, because you tend to feel, maybe not very consciously, that you can't just 'be yourself'. You have to have some achievement or social standing to back it up and,

in a sense, justify your existence (Ruler of first in tenth).

The picture is even more complicated than that and this basic front that you present is subject to a lot of stressful influence from other parts of your personality. It is not just a façade: the need to be lionized and looked up to, to express love and creativity in a big and dramatic manner, is essential to your deepest feelings of emotional security (Moon in Leo in 1). This itself is subject to a lot of stress and you will be inclined to behave in a discordant, obstinate way about your needs for attention and emotional support. You can behave very extravagantly indeed when you are feeling insecure but there is a strong sense of duty and professionalism that will usually keep you within bounds (Moon trine Jupiter sextile Saturn).

On top of that, the boundary between you and the world is unusually sensitive and impressionable. This has advantages in that it enables you to be intuitive and imaginative which, combined with your flair for the limelight, should amount to very considerable creative talent. However, it also means that you are never very clear about what exactly it is about yourself that you should be presenting. Other people are likely to find it hard to get a clear picture of you. You can put yourself over in an impressive and charismatic manner. This is obviously a plus point in many ways but it does mean that, for the most part, people are reacting and relating to an image of you rather than the reality. In the long run, this is bound to be unsatisfying.

2.   Similar remarks apply to your experience of having resources and a feeling of self-worth. Again, you need a lot of attention, to feel that you are outstanding, and to have some definite achievement to back up your feelings of self-worth. Money and material possessions will tend to have a rather theatrical, unrealistic quality for you. To some extent, this is because you feel that you don't really have the right to have money unless you've earned it and you never feel properly convinced that you've earned it (Ruler of second in tenth, Aries on tenth). This adds to your considerable sense of insecurity and anxiety. In most ways, however, money and possessions are not all that important an issue in themselves. It is in how they stir up other issues that they matter.

The best way for you to *make* money, at one level, and to nurture your feelings of self-worth at another, is to make full use of your creative and dramatic abilities. For all the insecurity, there is a very solid and substantial quality to you that should enable you to get tangible results from your creativity (Ruler in Taurus).

3.   The way you attempt to make sense out of what happens to you,

the way you think logically and put things together so that you know how to deal with life, is by being practical and critical. In some ways, you have a very sceptical mind; you want to examine all aspects of a matter before coming to a decision and you are deeply concerned with detail and routine. As far as possible, you like to have everything worked out beforehand. This is partly because you get confused easily and you are not very good at dealing with emergencies (Ruler square Neptune), partly from nervousness and a desire to be as prepared as possible (Ruler square Mars), and partly because you have a strong sense of professionalism and your criticisms and self-criticisms serve the purpose of strengthening your public image (Ruler in tenth). This kind of tough, critical, practical element in you is also a part of the way you present yourself to the world that we looked at in Phase 1 and it is something that other people will see in you quite strongly (Mercury square Ascendant).

4.   This next phase is another very basic one. It is your inner sense of personal identity that you have built up in response both to the outer pressures of life and your own inner needs. It is to do with your experience of belonging in your immediate environment and your ability to get support from it. To do this, you need harmonious surroundings and relationships. Harshness around you is very undermining. You are pretty tough, so you can deal with it, but persistent stress and harshness drains your nervous energy, which you do not easily replace.

Apart from harmonious one-to-one relationships and pleasant surroundings, you also need the experience of wider friendships and self-expression through groups in order to maintain a healthy sense of identity and belonging (Ruler in eleventh).

There is in this, however, an element of caution and defensiveness that makes it difficult for you to take in the expressions of friendship from others, even though you may be (and probably are) given them abundantly. It can be described as a distrust of intimacy and it may not be easy for you to accept compliments or other shows of approval which, of course, goes against the need for the limelight which we looked at earlier (Ruler trine Saturn).

On top of all this, the whole area of personal identity and sense of belonging is marked by a powerful sense of restriction. Soft and domestic feelings do not come readily to you. We may speculate that your early childhood was not particularly warm and loving but that such virtues as duty and work were much more emphasized. Whatever its origins, there is a considerable basic loneliness in your make-up that needs to be consciously acknowledged. If not, it may make its presence felt in the form of self-destructive behaviour (Ruler conjunct Pluto). Matters are complicated even further by the presence of a deep and intense part of yourself which underlies what you are normally able to see of your inner patterns (Intercepted Scorpio).

5.   We now move to the area of creative personal expression and the picture here is a bright one. You bring to creativity a great sense of exuberance and personal expansion. There is a way in which your creativity feeds on itself and is self-sustaining so that it can operate at full force even when there may be major difficulties in other areas of your life (Ruler in own sign and in house). You can be richly imaginative and, at the same time, popular and able to put yourself across to large numbers of people because of your ability to project a kind of basic humanity that they will recognize and accept (Ruler trine Neptune and Moon). In this area, you have a quick grasp of situations and a desire to develop your creativity through your own inner growth. Your intuition is powerful but may sometimes lead you astray since you are likely to be at times too dogmatic about it and you allow opposition to your ideas to make you stubborn.

6.   Your approach to work, in the sense of the routine matters that you have to deal with and the techniques of your job, is thorough and conscientious. You are also inclined to be somewhat conscious of status and position. You may strive to conceal this (Ruler in Libra) but you inwardly expect people to know their place. You put a great deal of energy into work. It brings out an assertive, innovative spirit in you. You can, however, be unusually restless and impatient with detail and routine and this is likely to provoke you into very stubborn and aggressive arguments which are all the more so because you are never really sure of the rightness of your own cause (Mars in sixth square Mercury opposite Neptune). This area of your life also relates to your ability to learn from mistakes and generally fit in with other people. You tend to be rather conscious of your deficiencies and worry about them but they are really too sore a point for you to be able to get into very thoroughly. Attempts to deal with them set off unresolved issues from childhood and raise uncomfortable questions about who you are and where you belong (Ruler in fourth).

7.   In one-to-one relationships you are very open, frank and engaging but surprisingly cool beyond a certain point. We have already noticed a certain distrust of intimacy. In relating to others, you are always watchful for the boundary between what you think proper and what

you consider should be private — that is, in terms of how much of your feelings you reveal (Rulers in fourth and eighth). In terms of what you say, you can be disconcertingly blunt and you are certainly not prudish (Mars conjunct Descendant square Mercury). Sexuality is not something that you feel very comfortable about. This is hardly surprising in view of the problems of identity and intimacy we have already discussed. Sexual feelings are strong but rather heavily blocked (Mars quincuncx Pluto) and so intimate relationships are loaded with a lot of tension. They tend to suffer, too, from a need that you have to be in control. You want a relationship to be on your terms and, one way or another, you will achieve that, though it may not be easy for you to recognize what you are doing.

8.   This brings us to the area of life which is to do with deep emotional involvement with other people and with things other than yourself. The experience of sex is related to this area and so are such matters as joint finances. Again, you have an attitude of distance. You are prepared to be frank and open about such matters in a general, abstract way but you hold back from much actual participation. As with the area of creative expression, though less happily perhaps, there is a self-sustaining element in this aloofness. It is very unlikely that another person would break it down; you would have to be prepared to examine it yourself and dismantle the barriers from inside. You may be tempted to see your aloofness as an important source of your creativity but this is illusory. At some level, you feel you have a deep need for your aloofness and it comes into play even in circumstances when, consciously, you would much rather it did not.

9.   Your attitude to what we may call philosophical questions — the 'why' of life — is impressionable, imaginative and confused. It is difficult for you to put much order into your thoughts, for although you see it as a very desirable thing to do, in practice it is difficult for you to find the patience and the discipline to do it. You are too easily seduced by your visions of how you feel life should be to consider very readily how it is. There is a certain practical danger in this because it goes with a conviction that there really is a place over the rainbow and that you will find it if you look hard enough. A big temptation is to try to find it through alcohol or other drugs. Another way in which this attitude may work is that you are constantly looking for opportunities to make it big. Some of this is healthy ambition and the natural desire to make the most of your talents. Some of it, however, is an unrealistic way of compensating for the feelings of not really belonging.

10.   This next area of life is a particularly important one for you. It is to do with your status in the world, your experience of public approval, the way you set about your career. You bring to this area of life attitudes of vigorous self-assertion. You are competitive and forceful and courageous in your approach to career matters. You are enterprising and willing to take risks but with an element of caution and commonsense that serves you well (Saturn opposite Aries M.C.). In the way that you present yourself to the world, you are able to express what you want for your career and do so forcefully and clearly (Ruler opposite Ascendant square Mercury). The potential for success in this combination is obvious. With powerful creative talent, plus the drive to make use of it, you can hardly fail to make your mark in some way. Some kind of public career is unusually important to you. There is a sense in which it is what you most want to do, what your main purpose in life is (Sun in tenth). You can bring to it much originality, an ability to innovate and do things differently (Sun sextile Uranus). You should find your best outlet in work that involves the creation of images in some way, especially if it provides a form of escapism or entertainment for people at large (Sun square Neptune; Neptune opposite Mars opposite Descendant conjunct Moon).

11.   The area of life which is to do with group activities, friendships and acquaintances in general brings out a talkative, versatile, amusing side of you. You should, generally, be 'a good mixer', able to turn on the charm and to be caring as well as affable (Venus in Cancer in eleventh). At the same time, career is never very far from your mind and, though you enjoy people for their own sake, the ones you find most rewarding are those who are in some way involved in things that matter, or may matter, for your career (Ruler in tenth). The only problem in this area is that you will need to watch your tendency to want to dominate and to be in control. You can sometimes alienate others in this way.

12.   The final area is the most mysterious one. It is to do with confronting your own deepest inner resources, your experience of intangible, non-worldly things. In some ways, it often has to do with being secluded or alienated from the world, either physically (as in staying in hospital) or in certain ways of being. In your case, the way you deal with this area of life is that you are self-protective about it on the one hand and very demonstrative of it on the other (Ruler in first). It is as though you have a great deal of hidden vulnerability which you want to keep to yourself, yet you almost brandish being a loner (Moon in first, conjunct Neptune; Neptune conjunct

Ascendant). It is a sort of letting people see some of your vulnerability — indeed, almost thrusting it upon them — as a way of masking and protecting much deeper and more sensitive levels of it.

To sum up your chart briefly, your potential for material success is very high and you have powerful creative gifts. There is, however, a lack of emotional contact and nurturing that makes the demands on you very heavy. Your tendency is to brush the issue aside, to put a good face on it and employ various forms of escapism. If you could bring yourself to explore the painful emotional lack you would be better able to control it.

6.
LIFE CATEGORIES IN SYNTHESIS

The 'houses' format of Chapter 5 is best suited for a psychological approach to the chart where you know that the client is accustomed to a certain amount of self-reflection. For the less psychologically sophisticated client a format involving a number of concrete categories may be more appropriate. This is the pattern developed by Margaret Hone and many readers may therefore already be familiar with it.

The Margaret Hone categories as she describes them, with their significators, are:[1]

1. *General characteristics*   Sun, Moon, first house, general chart formation.
2. *Mentality*   Third / ninth houses, fifth for creativity, eighth and twelfth for intuitional ability. Mercury and other planets for special abilities.
3. *Career, money, working ability*   Tenth for general career issues. Sixth for routine work. Jupiter and Saturn for success and obstacles. Seventh for partners and associates. Second / eighth for money.
4. *Spare-time occupations* First house. Fifth (pleasure). Sun, Moon, Ascendant ruler.
5. *Friends, love, marriage*   Eleventh, fifth, seventh, eighth. Venus for rapport, Mars for outreaching force. Sun in a woman's chart, Moon in a man's.
6. *Family contacts*   Moon, Saturn, fourth, tenth for mother and father. Third and Mercury for brothers and sisters. Fifth for children.
7. *Health*   First house. Sixth, twelfth for hospitalization. Sun for vitality and heart. Moon for functional disorders. Saturn for chills

[1] These categories are taken from Margaret E. Hone, *Applied Astrology*, London: Fowler (1953).

and falls; Mars — burns, scalds, cuts, fevers. Jupiter, liver trouble. Uranus — circulation, breaks, sprains.

8. *Travel* Third, ninth houses. Mercury and Jupiter.

The suggested categories provide a workable way of organizing the chart material though they need a certain amount of examination. Category 1, *General characteristics*, seems unexceptionable and setting out the information from Sun, Moon, Ascendant and planets in the first house under one broad heading is desirable. There is a tendency in practice for this section to get headed *Character*, which is too vague a term. Otherwise, we will take Category 1 as it stands.

Category 2, *Mentality*, seems to me a rather arbitrary division, at least without a little more explanation and discussion. In one sense mentality, if by that we mean general habits of mind, should come under *General characteristics*. In Chapter 5 I have partly defined the third and ninth houses as 'using one's mind to make sense of'. Mercury similarly has a purposeful, problem-solving type of energy. I suggest therefore that we keep this category of significators but call the category *Problem-solving abilities* rather than *Mentality*.

Category 3, *Career, money, working ability*, is fine as it stands except that Jupiter is linked too facilely with success. Jupiter is expansion and it is quite possible to expand in the wrong direction! Also, success and responsibility are often virtually synonymous and responsibility is certainly Saturn. Deductions about success and the obstacles to it from Jupiter and Saturn are, therefore, likely to be misleading. Nevertheless, these two planets, which are concerned with socio-economic status, obviously have to be considered. It will perhaps be safest to say that their placings show what the client finds easy and difficult in terms of career — the term 'working ability' is rather vague. The sixth house is about one's ability to learn the job and handle the routine. The second house should be considered here as showing the kind of personal resources one is able to bring to a career or job. We also need to add Mars for initiative. Let us change the category title to *Working life; career*.

One's attitude to and ability to handle money are important enough to deserve a separate category. Here we need to look at the second and eighth houses and Jupiter and Saturn again for spending and saving attitudes, and Venus for one's sense of value and attitudes to luxuries, personal comfort and adornment. We will call this category simply *Money*.

The next — *Spare-time occupations* — has a very plodding tone about it. It also seems rather futile, since presumably the client will know what hobbies he is interested in. Clearly, though, the category itself is useful since it enables us to deal with abilities that are not being used, or may not be being used, in the career. Let us rename the category *Creative talents* and add to the significators Venus, for pleasure in using the talents, and Mars for the drive and energy to do so.

Friends, love, marriage is an area we can be franker about than was possible in 1953. We can make two categories out of this and call them *Relationships* and *Sexuality*.

Relationships includes both strongly emotional and more impersonal relationships and refers to the day-to-day business of getting along with people. Significators are the seventh, eleventh, fifth and eighth houses. I would definitely include aspects to the North Node.

Sexuality refers to attitudes to one's own sexuality and ease or difficulty in expressing it. Significators are Venus and Mars, second, eighth and fifth houses. The second house is included because sexual energy is a personal resource.

Family contacts might be more usefully renamed *Family influences*. Moon and Saturn, by sign, house position and aspects, say more about how we *perceive* our parents than how they actually were. We need to notice that there is no general agreement about which house represents which parent. Some writers attribute the fourth to the mother and the tenth to the father — logically, it seems to me, considering the links with Moon and Saturn. However, other writers reverse this on what, they say, are empirical grounds. Perhaps the safest thing is to say that the combined fourth/tenth axis shows the combined parental influence. The significators for siblings and offspring can be retained (though obviously we need to make sure that the client has some before saying much about them!)

I doubt the wisdom of saying anything about Category 7, *Health*, to the average person. I question even more the accuracy and effectiveness of the advice that may be given. Unless the astrologer is a specialist in medical astrology, interpretations relating to specific health issues are going to be hit or miss. Moreover, the advice given is likely to be of the order of telling a strong Mars type that he is liable to headaches and should try not to get so tense about things, or a strong Saturn to try to guard against colds and chills. The advice may be pertinent, as far as it goes, but is almost totally useless.

Somewhat similar considerations apply to the last category, *Travel*. Travel is very important in the lives of some people; others have little interest in it. The client will usually know which category he belongs to without being told, so travel hardly seems to justify a category of its own. If it *is* clearly important in the chart, it can be mentioned under *Career* or *Creative talents*. A problem is that the indicators of travel — mainly emphasized ninth house, Sagittarius and Jupiter — might show a footloose wanderer or they might show someone who is content to stay at home and explore profound questions of philosophy and religion. Or we might have somebody who does both these things yet shows no very obvious sign of either from the chart (Albert Schweitzer, for example, who has only Venus in Sagittarius, semi-square to a first house Jupiter[2]).

Before we go on to an actual working with chart categories, let us tabulate the new ones for reference.

1. *General characteristics*   Sun, Moon, Ascendant, Midheaven.
2. *Problem-solving abilities*   Third and ninth, fifth for creativity, eighth, twelfth, Uranus and Neptune for intuition. Mercury for logic.
3. *Working life: Career*   Tenth for career status, sixth for learning and routine, second for personal resources. Mars for initiative. Jupiter for things that come easily, Saturn for difficulties. Seventh and North Node for partners and associates.
4. *Money*   Second and eighth for dealing with own and joint resources. Jupiter for spending, Saturn for saving. Venus for sense of values.
5. *Relationships*   Seventh, eleventh, fifth and eighth. Aspects to North Node.
6. *Sexuality*   Venus and Mars. Second, eighth and fifth.
7. *Family influences*   Moon and Saturn, fourth and tenth for influence of parents, Mercury and third for influence of siblings. Fifth for relations with children.
8. *Creative talents*   First house, Ascendant ruler. Sun, Moon. Fifth. Venus for enjoyment, Mars for drive and energy. (Ninth and Jupiter for any emphasis on travel.)

Since *General characteristics* comprises Sun, Moon, Ascendant and Midheaven, the four most personal points of the chart, it is useful to sub-divide this category and deal with them separately. They fall, for a start, naturally into the Sun/Moon, Asc./M.C. pairs. The first pair can broadly be said to relate to inner feelings and attitudes, the second pair to one's interactions with the world.

[2]Data: 14 January 1875, 11.50 p.m. GMT, Kayserburg, Alsace, 7 E 16, 48 N 09. Source: *American Book of Charts*.

The meaning of the Sun, for all that it is used so freely, is a little tricky to define exactly. It has the sense of overall purpose, the drive to have your life be a certain way and to conform to a more or less integrated view of yourself. It can therefore be said to be what you want and strive for.

The Moon is more what you already are, or perceive yourself to be inwardly. It is a set of already existing structures that enables you to deal with your life more or less automatically and maintain a sense of *inner* identity.

The Ascendant is the half-intuitive, automatic way in which you interact with other people and present yourself to them. It is a learned response based on your sense of what is going to work. It is the way other people see you, the impression you make at first meeting.

The Midheaven is also something you strive to be but it is probably the most conscious of all the four points. It is how you see yourself in terms of your public image, your status in the community.

We can therefore break down the *General characteristics* category further into:

How you want to be.
How you are.
How you relate to the world.
How you see yourself.

To illustrate the use of this format, we will work through Chart B again (Figure 2., p. 31), that of W. H. Auden. The aim here, as with the houses format of the last chapter, is to produce a written report that can be assimilated directly by the client. If you are really new to astrology, I would recommend making the preliminary breakdown notes as we did in Chapters 2 and 3. Once you are reasonably fluent in analysing a chart, however, you can dispense with doing this, at least as a preliminary to a fairly lengthy written or taped report.

ANALYSIS OF CHART B BY CATEGORIES

General Characteristics

How you want to be
This section describes the sense of overall purpose that you have for your life, not so much in specific ambitions but in the general aim that you have to be an integrated and consistent personality. It is the

way of being yourself that seems most natural and right to you. It is a part that is constantly being revealed and is constantly developing throughout your life and it generally begins to be most apparent after the age of about thirty.

(⊙ in ⌓) For you, this overall sense of how you should be is of being very open and impressionable. This makes you sensitive, intuitive and always aware of the need for some experience beyond the pressures of the everyday world. Many things will interest you and claim your attention and you may well possess not only considerable artistic sensitivity and talent but a bent for scientific matters as well.

You have a great capacity for enjoying life and it gives you particular pleasure to be with people. At the same time, you need to keep a private part of yourself closed off, even at the height of the party. This secret and private self is one that you will often want to retreat into, seeking solitude. Generally, secrecy and privacy are major characteristics in you. You tend to keep your affairs and problems to yourself and to admire others who can do the same. Every now and again, though, there is a demon of indiscretion who pops out in you and you will blurt out your own and other people's secrets in an amazingly open and incautious manner.

A difficulty that you have is that you are easily bored and constantly in search of some new sensation to enliven your life. If you allow this to get out of hand, you can be an unreliable hedonist, going along with whatever feels good and with little sense of responsibility towards what you have said you would do.

(⊙ in 4) Your home and a sense of belonging to an intimate group of people, whether family or friends, are very important to you. You are inclined to be sentimental and nostalgic; the friends that you made at school are likely to remain friends throughout your life. You probably have a considerable social conscience. You might present this to the world as being a matter of principle but it is really a sensitive and emotional sympathy for the underdog. Once you are committed to something, you will pursue it with great intensity and determination.

(⊙ ☐ ♂) You have access to plenty of energy and enthusiasm but are somewhat inclined to drive yourself too hard which may result in fits of exhaustion and depression. You may have a tendency to be dogmatic or inconsiderate which can be rather a burden to other people.

(⊙ △ ♃) You are abundantly gifted, creative, well-informed and you have a strong desire for recognition. There is, however, something of an easy-going playboy quality to all this and you will need to apply considerable self-discipline to make the most of your talents. There is also some tendency to be over-indulgent, for example, with food.

(☉ △ ♆) It is easy for you to escape into generalities rather than deal with particular problems that are in front of you, to strike attitudes rather than take action. In some ways, life comes easily to you because you never set yourself challenges that you cannot meet. This tendency to do what you know you will succeed at, combined with your powerful creative gifts, makes for a formidable force in your professional ambitions.

(☉ △ Asc.) The sense that you have of your overall purpose finds a ready expression in your way of presenting yourself to the world. The two combine to give you a powerful presence, easy and genial.

(☉ ⚻ ♋) Yet, there is some awkwardness and strain in the way you relate to others, especially those not close to you. There may be a tendency to superiority feelings, a general sense that other people are not, somehow, quite good enough.

How you are
This is the level of existing structures, the things that come automatically to you. The previous section, to some extent at least, described potential; this one describes patterns that have been set from early childhood.

(☽ in ♓) Insatiable curiosity is likely to be your main characteristic here. You have to *know* about things, to be in on the secret, and you get very uncomfortable if you are not. Here again, there is a great deal of enthusiasm but it tends to be more enthusiasm and activity for its own sake, rather than for any particular end. Almost certainly you will have a definite gift for words and considerable fluency in using them to express your ideas — *ideas*, not feelings. The tendency to conceal your personal feelings, which we looked at in the previous section, is not contradicted here. Indeed, at this level there is some tendency to block off feelings altogether and have as little as possible to do with them. There will be times when you can appear cold, detached and inconsiderate. You will rarely be less than intellectually stimulating but anyone who is looking to you for deep emotional commitment is likely to be disappointed. Again, at this level, you are very much the party type, able to carry on half a dozen conversations at the same time and to make original and witty comments into the bargain. If your thinking tends towards the glib and superficial, your brilliance of expression goes a long way to make up for it. Also, any lack of depth will be balanced by the sheer breadth of your knowledge and your ability to express it. You are not really very aware of your own motives and not <u>much interested</u> in them so you can have several distinct personalities without knowing it. Other people will know it, though!

($\mathbb{D}$ in 8) Now comes something of a counter-current to what has just been said. At this level of automatic given behaviour, you tend to get into circumstances where considerable intensity and commitment are called for and demanded of you. Whether you like it or not, you find yourself compelled to get to the roots of things; the rather light and casual attitude to the truth that has been evident so far is replaced by a much more serious and searching approach.

Although you do such a good job of shutting out your feelings for the most part, you nevertheless get into situations where you have to confront very passionate feelings, in yourself and other people. When this does happen your main reaction, probably, will be embarrassment and a rocklike mask of imperturbability. Then, you will probably channel the energies into your work and career in some way.

($\mathbb{D}$ □ ☿) In fact, the feelings that you attempt to control and reject do not go away; they hang around and interfere with your judgements. Although you place much importance on clarity and rationality, it is difficult to bring them to bear on your personal affairs. You can act in ways that seem afterwards to have been incredibly immature. Some of the difficulty lies in not being able to see the wood for the trees. You become preoccupied with the trivialities and miss the major issues. A result of this can be that you sometimes feel badly misunderstood by other people.

($\mathbb{D}$ □ ♄) This tendency is not helped by a further indication of rather severe suppression of feelings. It is as though your capacity for feeling were frozen below a certain level. There may well be a lot of guilt and a certain emotional dependence on others that is actually a fear of seeming to be disloyal.

($\mathbb{D}$ ♂ ♇) The repressed feelings can leap out very powerfully if you are in love. You are always looking for someone who can respond to you totally. Once you are in love, you can be very demanding and possessive. Sex is extremely important to you but we will look at it in detail under the appropriate heading.

How you relate to the world
This level is a kind of automatic colouring that you adopt in the way that you present yourself to other people.

(Asc. ♏) As we have already seen, it is linked in a harmonious way with the level of overall purpose and this gives you an element of confidence, power and geniality. Indeed, power and presence are the words that most readily spring to mind in describing this aspect of you. There is great strength and endurance in you and a sense of hidden reserves. No one is likely to think of you as being shallow, in spite of the verbal glibness and dexterity that we looked at earlier.

There is a definite charisma about you and, given the right sort of opportunities, you can have a considerable influence in the world. You convey a feeling of seriousness and substance, as if you are not afraid to pursue a matter to its depths and follow through on all its implications. As on other levels, though, we again see a certain degree of emotional reserve and you may sometimes appear to be cold and aloof.

Another negative possibility at this level is a certain degree of intolerance. It is not that you are indifferent to other people's pain and suffering — far from it, you are liable to feel it all too keenly. You do, however, expect everyone to be as tough as yourself and to be able to deal with their troubles on their own — their emotional troubles, anyway.

(Asc. △⊙) Again, the characteristics on this level are very promising for success. You have, or can muster, enough willpower, patience, insight and persistence to succeed at anything you commit yourself to. And you do commit yourself to things. You are virtually never lukewarm. You are either involved in something heart and soul or you are not interested at all.

(Asc. ☐ ☊) If people look carefully underneath the first impression of power, they may see some kind of emotional damage. Part of the image of power that you present you have developed in order to compensate for, though not quite conceal, some weakness. It tends to add to the air of guardedness and defensiveness that you project.

(Asc. ⊔ ☿) Again, you are likely to be very verbal and to use words as a smokescreen to cover up your feelings or, perhaps, lack of feelings. You may have a tendency to grumble and complain a good deal, finding fault with yourself and others. There may also be a rather amoral element in you and you are inclined to take the view that a course of action is justified if it works or if you can get away with it. This, of course, is rather at odds with the strong sense of responsibility and concern for principle that you otherwise have.

(Asc. △ ♃) Generally, people fascinate you and you are mostly open and expansive towards them, generous with your time and energy. You may, however, sometimes offend, or at least disconcert, others by taking a large and Olympian view which they feel, in the circumstances, to be inappropriate. It can look as though you are being casual and dismissive about something your listeners regard as serious.

(Asc. ⊔ ♄) In fact, you do generally give the impression that you regard life as being a serious matter. There are times when you can be gloomy and pessimistic, when you lose your nerve with people and feel hesitant and inadequate. Generally, you act with a strong sense of propriety, perhaps even carrying it to the point of being rather rigid in your views and attitudes.

How you see yourself
This section describes a part of you that is fairly easily accessible to your conscious reflection about yourself. It is, in a sense, how you want other people to see you, as distinct from the last section, which is how they actually *do* see you. It is your public image and therefore has a strong bearing on your career and professional life. However, we will look at that in another section and concentrate here on the personal and psychological characteristics of this level.

(M.C. ♌) Here, you definitely see yourself as the leader. Your natural place is in the limelight and you shouldn't have to fight to get there, either. You are certainly proud, ambitious and highly motivated — even driven — to success, and yet you have the feeling that such success and the resulting admiration is no more than your natural due. There is something rather medieval and heroic about your own image of yourself and you have a strong sense of chivalry and *noblesse oblige.*

This is an image that usually enables you to act in a confident, self-assured matter, even when you are not feeling that way. It gives you a flair for the dramatic; you probably appreciate and enjoy theatre and you can be not a little theatrical yourself, especially when something has upset you. It is not easy for you to share the limelight. If you feel that someone has intruded upon it, or has not shown you the deference and appreciation that you were expecting, you are liable to let them know in a forceful way.

At this level, you are liable to see things in black and white; people are either good or bad, heroes or villains. You have a tendency to cling very firmly to idealistic notions about how things are or ought to be, which means that you are frequently disconcerted by the impact of real life. This is at odds with the very fluid and flexible view of the world that you have at the level of overall purpose. These two different qualities can serve as useful counters to each other. The more you can become aware of them, the better your chances of using them to moderate each other, rather than to conflict.

(M.C. Δ ♂) As we have described it so far, your conscious image of yourself is powerful but inclined to be a bit static. There is, however a blending in of drive and initiative that will tone down the sense of having an absolute right to power and admiration and give you more awareness that it is something that you also have to go out and get. This obviously, is another very powerful success combination.

(M.C. ⚻ ♅) There is too a distinct originality, even eccentricity, about your public image. It amounts to a certain pleasure in unexpectedly going against the grain of events. This element in you can be a powerful attention-getting device but it may sometimes have a self-sabotaging effect. You may have a tendency to do something odd or eccentric just for the sake of it in ways which may be inappropriate and which do not contribute to your own interests.

(M.C. ⚺ ♆) Finally, in order to really muster energy for your public image, you need to have goals that catch your imagination and, for all the powerful ego that is present at this level, you need to have a sense of dedication to something larger than merely personal goals. If you can find something to dedicate yourself to, you will create a very impressive and charismatic public personality.

Problem-solving Abilities

(♑ on 3) The task of making sense of your immediate experiences and learning how to relate effectively to the world is something that you take seriously. You will also feel that your ability to do it has a bearing on your sense of social status. You are aware of your own intelligence and capacity but sometimes feel undermined by inner insecurity (♄ in 4). You perhaps do not always think as clearly and rigorously as you might and sometimes you are inclined to accept general solutions to problems which do not really deal with the issues but which provide you with a sense of emotional security (♋ on 9). You will not, however, be entirely satisfied with these solutions because you will always have a sense of there being deeper roots to the matter, even if you do not wish to explore those roots (☽ in 8). Intuition and capacity for inspiration are very powerful — perhaps uncomfortably so — and you will often tend to deal with your intuitions in a logical way, which is not very appropriate (♓ on 5; ☽ ☌ ♇ in 8; ♀ ☌ ♅; ☽ in ♊).

Nevertheless, if you allow you intuition to speak for itself, you will find that you can give it very tangible form, most likely in writing (♉ on 8). This is particularly important since the ideas and feelings which come to you in solitude will demand some kind of harmonious display and presentation to other people (♎ on 12). There is an implication here that you may be inclined to tone them down too much and make them too 'presentable'.

In general, although you will probably be able to create the impression that you are a logical and analytical thinker, you are not really so at all, being quite undisciplined and too apt to be satisfied with generalities about life instead of really observing your experiences closely.

Working Life: Career
(M.C. ♌) We have already seen that your sense of public image is majestic and dramatic and you will be happiest if you can pursue some career or profession that will enable you to satisfy the needs involved. It is not just a question of being a leader and getting recognition for achievement. That is certainly important but there is also a powerful need for personal creativity; you need to be able to put your unmistakeable personal stamp on whatever you do.

(♈ on 6) Whatever it is, it should not be something that demands a great deal of routine nor something that requires you to spend long periods sitting at someone else's feet. You are the type that needs to learn by doing and you are too eager to get on with it and too impatient of other people's ideas to make a good pupil. If you set your *own* tasks, it is a different matter.

(♐ on 2) The kind of resources you are able to bring to your career consist of a capacity for absorbing and using a wide range of knowledge and learning. Broadly, too, this kind of wide-ranging field is what is most likely to excite your initiative and get you moving (♂ in ♐).

(♃ in ♋ in 8) What will come easily to you professionally is the ability to gather groups of supportive people around you who will not only support you as a friend but who will appreciate the deeper values of what you are doing. Obviously, this is a considerable asset. What will be difficult is precisely that sense of being dedicated to a specific goal that we have already looked at (♄ in ♓). In general, it will be hard for you to deal with large issues without feeling overwhelmed by them but you do not have the patience and capacity for detail to take them a piece at a time. You will have a tendency, therefore, to adopt a kind of broad-brush style in your work which often successfully glosses over the fact that you have not thought it out very fully. Your impatience with routine and need for quick results do not augur very well for a business career, except perhaps in the more creative echelons of advertising or public relations. Acting or writing are the kind of things that immediately suggest themselves.

(♀ on 7) If you are involved in any kind of partnership it needs to be one that you can trust and feel committed to because you will be reluctant to make changes even if it is going wrong. In general, your capacity for associating with others is a little off-beat and off-beam and you would probably be best advised to operate essentially on your own, at least as far as any formal partnership is concerned (hard aspects to ☊).

Money
(♃ and ♄ in water) Your attitude to money is not likely to be especially practical. In particular, you may react to lack or shortage of money by glossing over or ignoring it rather than by taking action. You may be tempted to spend more than you ought out of a sense of self-indulgence (♄ in ♓). There may be a feeling that spending money provides some sort of emotional comfort (♃ in ♋). It might be interesting to see whether in fact you are inclined to spend more freely when you are feeling low emotionally. Generally, your sense of values is a fairly conventional one and you will be more or less conformist in your attitudes to money and what it can do (♀ in ♉), though you may have a few eccentricities about it (♀ ☌ ♅).

(♏ on 2) You will be inclined to be somewhat secretive about money, especially when it is to do with your own resources. In dealing with joint resources or other people's money, e.g. bank loans, you will be, again, conventional, reliable and disinclined to make changes in existing arrangements (♇ on 8).

Relationships
(♍ on 11) In some ways your attitude to relationships in the sense of friendships is a very intellectual one. You will be to some extent inclined to develop friendships because there are good *reasons* to do so as much as from any great personal attraction to the people concerned. At the same time, you will be inclined to value your friends for their intellectual gifts and accomplishments and you can be rather critical and choosy in this regard.

(♇ on 7) When you have formed a close one-to-one relationship with someone, you will see it as a major source of stability in your life and you will want it to be an enduring arrangement, even though you may not be particularly faithful or constant (♓, ♓). You will probably develop a gift for relationships in which both you and your partner(s) have a good deal of freedom yet continue to preserve the essential arrangement (♀ ☌ ♅; ♇ on 8). This will become more difficult for you once you get beyond a certain degree of emotional commitment and you may tend to avoid such commitment for that reason (☽ ☌ ♇ in 8).

(♓ on 5) So far as relationships have an element of pleasure and recreation, you will be idealistic about them, able to let go and enjoy yourself and to be carried away by whatever is going on.

Sexuality

There is a basic conflict in your approach to sexual relationships. As far as the emotional aspect of sex is concerned, you are rather conventional, somewhat subdued and desirous of doing the proper thing (♀ in ♉). The physical side of sex is quite different (♂ in ♐). Here, you will be much more inclined to go for what you want in a direct manner. Probably more than most people, you are able to separate the two sides of sex and to enjoy purely physical sex in an uninhibited way. It may be, even, that it is actually necessary for you to feel no emotional attachment or obligation to a partner in order to enjoy sex and that, as soon as you become emotionally involved with someone, all kinds of complications arise (♂□♄). This does indeed create difficulties because even with a completely satisfying physical relationship you will feel frustrated unless there is emotional contact (☽ ♂ ♇).

(♋ on 5) As with relationships in general, you are able to lose yourself in sexual pleasure and, in fact, pleasure tends to dominate a good deal of your life. You are inclined to see sexual activity as something necessary for your emotional stability and physical health (♅ on 8; ♏ on 2). Your feelings about your sexual energy as a personal resource are intense and passionate, though you may be able to make light of them (☽ in ♋ in 8). In general, sex is extremely important in your life; more important, in some ways, than love. At any rate, it is much less of a problem; it comes more naturally and easily to you than love does.

Family Influences

(☽ □ ♄) It is likely that there is some conflict in you that stems, in part, from a conflict at some level between your parents. The chart shows how you experienced your parents rather than how they necessarily were and you must have experienced very different influences from them. You seem to have perceived your mother as being lively, nervous and intense, extremely emotional in a sense but with the emotion being mostly self-absorbed, perhaps in anxiety, and which has left a corresponding tendency to nervousness and anxiety in you (☽ in ♋ in 8; ☽□♀ ♂ ♇). It seems unlikely that she was very affectionate or demonstrative.

(♄ in ♋) In contrast, your father seems to have been the more affectionate of the two, gentler and more easy-going, though still inclined to keep a good deal of emotional distance from you. It seems possible that if your father exemplified what are usually regarded as feminine qualities (to you, that is) and your mother exemplified the more traditionally masculine ones, you may yourself be confused about sexual roles.

(≈ on 4; ♌ on 10) In general, your parents would have emphasized the importance of pride in oneself yet humanitarian concern for others. Both would, in their different ways, have seemed to you to be solid and rather rigid in the ways in which they related to you. A lot of your later life may have been conditioned by the need to find some similar firm and solid set of circumstances.

The influence of any brothers or sisters would have been in the direction of conforming to the rules and stressing the importance of social status and achievement (♄ on 3). There is, however, also an element of idealism and romanticism involved (☿ in ♓).

(♓ on 5) If you have children of your own, you will again tend to be idealistic about them. You will be something of a perfectionist yet at the same time perhaps not a very good disciplinarian.

Creative Talents
It will be evident from what has already been said that you should have considerable creative talents. If circumstances have been helpful, you have probably discovered them and made them into the basis of a career. Perhaps there is not much more to add except to comment that you will be strongly motivated to use these gifts and, to some extent, using them will be as much an act of self-assertion as of creation (♂ in ♐ ; ☉ □ ♂ ; ☿ □ ♂). At the same time, you will have a strong sense of responsibility to your gifts and you will enjoy polishing them and what will often be the sheer hard work of using them (♀ in ♄).

We can see how this categories format lends itself to — indeed positively invites — a lengthy and fairly discursive style in a way which the others do not. It is, therefore, particularly suitable for mail order work for clients who are not accustomed to dealing with information about themselves and who expect a lot of detail. This is why the format has been so popular. It is also an excellent exercise for beginning astrologers because it stretches them to put down as much as they know and yet provides a framework which is sufficiently tight to make sure that they keep control of their material.

Without a prodigious memory any astrologer will be more or less compelled to use some kind of text in doing this type of report, if only as an *aide-mémoire*. What to leave out and when to stop can then become problems. To some extent, this has to be an individual decision but I would suggest that the example report is about the right length. A client who has paid a substantial fee for a written report would hardly expect less. On the other hand, the temptation to go on elaborating with more and more detail has to be resisted.

Every astrological factor can be written about at as much length as the astrologer has patience and imagination for (as witness those popular books which have twenty or thirty pages dedicated to each sign). One thing that needs to be remembered here, though, is that the more concrete detail one puts down, without being able to check it with the client, the more likely it is that individual details will be wrong. If they are not actually wrong, they may be worded in such a way that the client does not recognize them and cannot assimilate them, in which case they might as well be wrong. A useful limitation is built into the chart itself in that it becomes repetitious beyond a certain point. If we find ourselves saying the same thing over and over again, we are putting in too much. Even so, a certain amount of repetition is inevitable in this style of report and is even a good idea from the point of view of the client. The whole technique is exactly the opposite of the themes technique. With the themes, we are seeking to boil the information down as much as possible as a preliminary to a thorough discussion with the client. With the categories report, we have no means of checking the client's reaction and so it is desirable to say the same thing two or three times. What I am advising against is saying the same thing five or six times!

In the chart we have just used there is some doubt as to whether the Ascendant is Scorpio or Libra. I have chosen to assume that the birth time is correct and written the report as though the Ascendant were definitely Scorpio. Photographs and biographical details of Auden do seem appropriate to a Scorpio Ascendant.

If a similar problem arises in real life we can either attempt to rectify the chart from events, which can be time-consuming without being conclusive, or we can ask for a photograph to see if that will give a clue as to which of two Ascendants is the right one. Failing either of these, I suggest saying plainly in the report what the problem is and giving half the Ascendant, or M.C., section to one sign and half to the other, inviting the client to decide which fits. I am very doubtful of the validity of the idea of 'cusps' applied to signs and I do not think there is an overlap effect. Either the planet or angle is in the sign or it is not. I have a strong suspicion that the idea of a cuspal effect that blends the qualities of both signs was invented by newspaper astrologers so as not to lose their readers who do not know what Sun-sign they are.

7.
THE ROLE OF PREDICTION

The use of natal astrology for psychological diagnosis is now reasonably well understood and can be regarded as reliable. If we bear in mind the existence of the spectrum of meaning of astrological factors and do not get stuck in a limited form of interpretation, it can be almost totally reliable. My view is that this *is* what astrology is about — its chief function is to assist people in the very difficult task of seeing themselves clearly and making unconscious issues conscious.

There is a considerable body of opinion, particularly amongst those whose only contact with astrology is via newspaper columns, that astrology's chief function is to predict the future. Can astrology in fact predict the future? And if it can what good does this do? How can we use it?

The issue of prediction is a tricky one and its current practice rests on some assumptions about the nature of the universe and about life that are not usually examined. If they are, they turn out to be rather shaky. My own conclusions about the value of predictive techniques and their correct use are not nearly so clear as my perceptions about analytical natal work. I am not, therefore, proposing anything definitive in this chapter about where prediction fits into chart synthesis. What I want to do is open up some issues that are usually glossed over or ignored so that we can begin to take another look at prediction.

First of all, does it work? If I rely on my own experience, my answer has to be 'No — and yet there seems to be *something* in it.' I cannot recall a single prediction that has ever been made for me on the basis of my chart that has ever worked out in a clear and unambiguous manner. Predictions made on the basis of Tarot readings or clairvoyance have a slightly better score, but not much. I can think of maybe three predictions made by Tarot readers or clairvoyants that have come about more or less as forecasted. Of these, only one can be said to have worked out fully. On the other hand, really major turning-points in my life have gone unmentioned, even though they were within the time span that the reader was considering. Magazines and newspapers often have features of predictions for the year made by famous psychics. These predictions almost never come about or, if they do, they could have been predicted in the ordinary way by extrapolation from current trends. Presumably, it is only the fact that newspaper and magazine readers forget what they have read within a few days that enables these famous 'seers' to retain any shred of reputation. That, and the fact that they may do better with their individual clients.

Most books on astrological prediction are written from the standpoint that astrology works in the rather uncomplicated fashion that it is supposed to, i.e., that when a planet in the natal chart is aspected by a transiting, progressed or solar-arc-directed planet, events (or states of mind) corresponding to the nature of the two planets and of the aspect formed will take place. Thus, a transit of Mars conjunct Jupiter will be said to be excellent for physical activity; health and energy will be high and there will be the inclination to take risks and make them pay off. On the other hand, the transit of Mars opposite Neptune will mean feeling low and discouraged, encounters with others are likely to be disappointing and it is best to take life easily until the transit has passed. Similar interpretations would apply if it were progressed or solar-arc-directed Mars that was involved rather than the transiting planet.

This is fine as far as it goes and it is a correct deduction from the nature of the planets and the transiting aspects. But is it what actually happens in practice? There are three points which need to be made which this type of prediction does not take into account. One is astrological. The other two are a matter of general observation. Taking the matters of general observation first, it is evident that some people are much more event-prone than others. Some people live their lives in a whirlwind of activity and even crisis. Something is always happening to them and often it is highly dramatic. Then there are people who, externally at least, live their lives on pretty much an even keel; for them two or three major events in a year would be a lot.

I am not sure what the explanation is but it seems to have something to do with whether people see their feelings or their mental processes as central to their life. If it is feelings, then the person will live what a certain disc jockey refers to as an 'action-packed' existence. The other kind of person, who values thinking rather than feeling, will have relatively little external activity. Actually, it is not so much a matter of valuing as of identifying with. In terms of the subpersonality theory, the 'central club' consists primarily of feeling subpersonalities in the one case and thinking subpersonalities in the other.

I have no really hard evidence but it seems to me likely that the feelings, high external-activity people are the ones who will be most likely to respond to transits, progressions, etc. in a fairly unambiguous way and with appropriate actual events. The thinking, low external-activity people are more likely to respond in terms of states of mind which will be a good deal more elusive and difficult to recognize.

The second general observation is that there seem to be people who do not respond to transits or progressions in the way they are supposed to at all. Actually, this includes just about everybody from time to time. Even people who find that transits or progressions click off their chart quite regularly will find that some go by without any detectable effect. What are we to think of that? Perhaps that there is some effect in the unconscious? That may be so and there is some reason to think so. Sometimes a major transit or progression will go by with neither an event nor an appropriate state of mind to show for it. Then, months later, something apt will occur. It may be that the person was simply not ready to confront the issues of the transit or progression consciously at the time that it happened astronomically. That is the kind of explanation that is, necessarily, somewhat suspect because it cannot be proved one way or the other. Nevertheless, something of this sort may happen, which must at least make us pause in our thinking about predictive work.

Those are the two general observations. The astrological one is a point that an older generation of astrologers insisted upon but which seems to be getting lost in the instant, throw-away, computerized atmosphere of much current astrological practice. As stated in older books, it is: 'Nothing can come about that is not shown in the natal chart'. It is obvious, really. To go back to our transiting Mars examples, if the chart as a whole shows the person to be heavy, indecisive and inhibited, no amount of Mars transiting Jupiter is going to suddenly turn him into a high energy ball of fire. Conversely, if he *is* a high energy ball of fire, transiting Mars opposite Neptune is not going to slow him down to any noticeable extent. The first person might be a little more optimistic than usual and the second person a little more sensitive than usual. In neither case would a blanket interpretation or advice based solely on the planets directly involved in the transit be of much use. Yet, by implication at least, this is what we are expected to believe from the way prediction is usually taught and written about.

Partly, I think, this misconception of prediction comes about from the pressure of clients who want to be told what is going to happen and do not want to take the time or make the effort (which *is* considerable) to find out what is already so about themselves. It is obvious that what will be so for a person in the future *must* be a development of what is so now. Secretly, what such clients really want to be told is that something will happen to solve their problems and make their lives wonderful without their having to do anything about it. Unfortunately, there really is no Santa Claus!

Prediction, therefore, must take second place to a thorough natal analysis. It is absurd to think of it as something in itself that can be divorced from any self-awareness on the part of the client. Apart from any other consideration, predictions based solely on the aspects made by transiting or progressed planets are bound to be hit or miss, as we have seen. We must take the whole chart into consideration, and also the entire condition of the planet that is being aspected. It simplifies matters to consider that what is important is more the kind of natal configuration that is being activated rather than the transiting or progressed planet and the nature of the aspect it is making. So, for example, all transits, progressions or solar-arc-directions to the Sun in a chart would be regarded as essentially the same. That is, they will primarily be stirring up the issues that the Sun, with its sign and house position and aspects, represents. The transiting or progressed planet represents the kind of stimulus that is being applied.

To take an example, suppose the chart indicates a certain tendency to shyness and withdrawal. This might be shown, among other things, by Moon in Scorpio in the twelfth, conjunct Saturn or Neptune. Let us suppose we are talking about a male chart. On one day our hypothetical male gets stopped by a policeman for speeding. Next day, he meets a pretty girl at a party. The two situations are as different as they well could be yet on both occasions he is likely to find that basic defensiveness is an issue he has to deal with in some way. In terms of actual transits, these two events might be represented by, say, a Saturn square for the policeman and a Venus conjunction for the pretty girl.

Another man has Moon in Aries in the fifth, square to a Jupiter/Uranus conjunction. If the same transits produced the same situations he would react very differently from the man in the first example. It would be more likely to be issues of assertion and aggression that were stirred up rather than withdrawal.

This, it seems to me, indicates the use of predictive techniques in synthesis. Their value is not so much in attempting to forecast what is going to happen but in throwing light on what is actually happening at the time the transits or progressions occur. The personality patterns represented by the excited natal configurations are being highlighted and are available for examination.

A case in point is that of a client who asked me what was going on in her chart because she was feeling very irritable and had had a major row with her son. The only activity in the chart was transiting Mars conjunct Venus. Almost any astrologer, looking at that ahead of time, would say that there would be some kind of romantic or sexual encounter. In this chart, Venus is in Pisces and the sixth house, opposite Neptune, square Jupiter, sesquiquadrate Pluto, square M.C. and conjunct Sun. This, it is true, suggests a powerful romantic and sexual subpersonality. However, another major theme of the chart is a great emphasis on independence and separateness. Sun, Mercury and Mars are in Aquarius and Moon is quincunx Uranus. The basic sexual and creative impulse of transiting Mars conjunct Venus has, in the first place, to contend with confusion and exaggeration, with the hard aspects to Neptune, Jupiter and Pluto. Though in some respects Venus in Pisces is a happy placing, it is also one that means it is difficult to be clear about one's affections and values. The sixth-house placing means that romantic feelings are liable to be brought down to earth and confined in an irritating way.

On top of that, the impulse has to work against a strong desire to maintain independence and detachment. So it is not surprising that a nebulous but powerful irritability was the result. As for the specific event of having a row with her son, he was, given the circumstances, the most likely person to attract her anger.

When we look at the chart in full and know the person's circumstances and psychological patterns, we might perhaps have predicted something of the kind. More useful, though, is to have the client look at her sexual frustration which arises from the incompatible drives for involvement and independence.

In general, it is pretty safe to say that if there are serious conflicts shown in the chart, even the most technically positive transit or progression is not going to resolve them. Bearing this in mind will enable us to avoid unrealistically optimistic predictions. Unrealistically pessimistic predictions should be avoided anyway. Some of the older books are inclined to exaggerate the effect of difficult Saturn, Uranus and Pluto aspects. An aspect may be difficult in itself and the natal configuration may be stressful, as in the above example. People still have a lot of channels available to them for using the energy and what looks like a dire transit may in fact have a positive and constructive result.

I have spoken so far mainly about transits because transits, of all the predictive techniques, seem to me to work most clearly. Secondary progressions, in my experience, have a much less substantial effect. I emphasize that this is only my own experience and I know that other astrologers find secondary progressions powerful. This seems to be one of the highly personal things about astrology, like the way one house system is tailored to one astrologer's style rather than another's.

The suggestion that transits refer to outer events and progressions to inner development appears to me to be unwarranted. Certainly transits can relate to both. This suggestion springs from the idea that transits are less 'symbolic' than progressions since we are dealing with the actual positions of the planets in the sky. But the aspects they make to the natal chart are just as symbolic as those of the progressed planets. There is nothing actually physically there for them to be aspecting. Indeed, as R. C. Davison[3] has pointed out, transits can be regarded as a type of progression in which 1 day = 1 day, rather than 1 day = 1 year, so there is no essential distinction between the two systems.

I have referred to solar arc directions. This is a technique derived from secondary progressions that frequently works very clearly. We find the difference between the secondary progressed Sun and the natal Sun for the day in question and add this difference to all the planets (tables are available to simplify the procedure). Some astrologers add the solar arc to the Ascendant, M.C. and intermediate house cusps. Doing this gives an astronomical monstrosity and other astrologers prefer to add the solar arc direction to the M.C. only and then calculate the directed Ascendant and intermediate house cusps from the new M.C. Again, students should check out both methods and decide for themselves which one suits them best. The fact that the first method produces a chart which is astronomically impossible does not invalidate it. The planetary positions produced by solar arc directions are impossible too. Other astronomically impossible charts, such as composites and harmonics, definitely work so there is no reason why house cusps advanced by the direct addition of the solar arc should not also work.

In theory, to get a full picture of what is going on at a given period, we should get out all the transits, solar arc directions and secondary progressions, paying attention to semi-square aspects, sesquiquadrates and quincunxes as well as the major aspects. Perhaps we should look at semi-sextiles too. Most writers are inclined to treat the semi-sextile as weak and unimportant but I am not at all sure that this view is

[3]R. C. Davison. *The Technique of Prediction*, London: Fowler (1955).

correct. After all, the semi-sextile is 'the other half' of the quincunx and the quincunx itself is becoming increasingly recognized as a powerful aspect, perhaps worthy to be classed as equivalent to the square and opposition.

This is what should be done in theory. In practice, I find that looking at the transits, taking into account the so-called minor aspects, is enough. For the major aspects we can allow larger orbs than most books suggest, at least if the purpose is not prediction as such but obtaining information on current developments. So, if we are doing some work for a client and we want to see what the current developments are, we can certainly look at transiting aspects up to 5° from exact, even 10°, for the conjunction, square and opposition, but not more than 3° for the minor aspects and the trine and sextile.

It remains true that, as most books say, the orb of major effectiveness of a transiting aspect is within 1° of exactitude. This is certainly when any appropriate definite *event* is likely to occur, if one does. However, an approaching aspect is like an approaching train. If we are listening for it, we can hear the rumble long before it pulls into the platform. So, using transits at these wider orbs gives us an opportunity to look at trends that are forming before they are on top of us. It has the added advantage that, for the faster transiting planets such as Mars, it extends the period over which we can be learning from the transit. With the usual orbs, a Mars, and even a Jupiter, transit can be over almost before we know what has happened, especially if there is no clear cut accompanying event.

8.
THE BASIC SYMBOLISM OF ASTROLOGY

So far, the methods of laying out the chart information that we have looked at have been time-consuming. They have all been essentially written methods. In the case of the houses format and the categories format, the writing has been intended as an end in itself and the report as it stands is sent to the client. In Chapter 10 we shall consider yet another format based on planetary phases and the same comments will apply. The themes format is different in that it is intended not as an end in itself but as the preliminary to a face-to-face discussion and we shall be considering the use of the themes in the actual session later. The process of discovering the themes, however, involves a lot of writing.

After all the practical applications we have worked through there is perhaps some danger of becoming overwhelmed by the detail and it is worth reminding ourselves of the principle stated in Chapter 1, i.e., organization of the chart material is not synthesis. It is a necessary first step but synthesis can only take place in the client's mind when he assimilates the information in such a way that it becomes a part of him and makes a difference to the way in which he perceives his life. To restate what was said earlier, the client's ability to synthesize the information depends on many things. One of the problems that we have to contend with is that everyone has a powerful investment in staying the way he or she is. A man may say that, for example, he wants to improve his relationships with women or do better in his career. If, however, his relationships with women are consistently unhappy or he stays in a job well below his capacities then we can be sure that he has a secret agreement with himself to be a failure. This agreement will almost certainly be secret from *himself* and, however brilliant our written analysis it will not get to the root of the failure pattern.

Such issues belong properly to the subject of counselling and a detailed examination of them is outside the scope of this book. However, since they have such a powerful bearing on the synthesis of material as we have defined it here, it is appropriate to look briefly at how such patterns arise and we shall do that in Chapter 11.

In this chapter we shall consider some of the problems involved in doing a face-to-face session without preliminary notes. I am convinced that if we want to work with (in the sense of counselling) our clients, it is better in fact to *have* preliminary notes. The reasons are two. First, the chart interpretation has been worked on beforehand so we are confident about it and reasonably sure that we have not missed out something important. Second, we can therefore focus all our attention on the discussion of the information and on the client.

Nevertheless, an essential part of the training of any astrologer should include learning to pick up a chart from scratch and do a decent job of interpreting it directly to the client. If you prefer to work as purely a giver of information, rather than as a counsellor, the situation is not much different from doing a written or tape recorded report and there is therefore less objection to a focusing a major part of your attention on the chart during the interview.

It sometimes happens that a potential client will call out of the blue and say that he is passing through town and can only come right now, or the next day. In these circumstances, you can either turn the client away or fit him in with barely enough time to set up the chart, let alone make elaborate notes on it. If you are in the early stages of building up a practice, it is sensible to see the client. It is not a good idea to turn away legitimate business and the experience of doing a session in such circumstances is invaluable. Even if you prefer to make preliminary notes, it is an effective training exercise to do the session with only your own knowledge and skill to rely upon, plus whatever inspiration and intuition may be going. Even experienced astrologers feel a surge of adrenalin in such situations. If you are new to astrology, it is probably better to try out your skills on a sympathetic friend first.

There are a number of tricks to help with instant chart reading. These include focusing on Sun, Moon and Ascendant for the major characteristics, paying a lot of attention to the overall shape of the chart and the preponderance or lack of elements and qualities. These are all useful dodges, up to a point, but if you rely on them, they will eventually let you down.

The only key to being a proficient instant chart reader is to really know your stuff, which means a good deal of reading, experience and general hard work. I suggested in an earlier chapter that every serious astrologer should aim to produce (or at least aim to be in a position to produce) his or her own personal interpretation manual. Although, as a beginner, you have to accept the other people's meanings of chart factors, you should use them as a kind of scaffolding for creating your *own* meanings. It is not that your meanings will be very different — in fact, they *shouldn't* be very different — but they will be *yours*. You will know them, experience them and feel them in a way you cannot with a memorized list of meanings from a textbook. You will know them well enough to be able to move about the spectrum of meaning of each factor rather than stick rigidly to a few keywords.

Some of this skill, of course, will only come as a result of experience and seeing how the delineations of chart factors work out in practice. This is another reason for doing a good proportion of off-the-cuff interviews. Mail order work alone gives little feedback on how accurate your interpretations are. And, as we have seen, the more detailed and concrete an interpretation is, the more likely it is to be wrong for a given client. Conversely, the more abstract the delineations, the more likely the client is to recognize and respond to them. Working by interview helps to develop a sense of balance and of what is appropriate to the person you are working with.

Let us take a hypothetical example. You are working with a male client whose chart has a Venus/Mars/Pluto conjunction in Leo. You say something like, 'Well, you're tremendously sexy and creative, you're very generous and loving with your girlfriends and you expect a lot of warmth and praise and absolute loyalty in return.' The response is a blank stare because the client does not resonate to any of this. He is actually somewhat dignified and aloof, considers he has an obligation to restrain his sexual feelings and feels he is really rather above that sort of thing anyway!

Your interpretation of the Venus/Mars/Pluto conjunction in Leo is certainly not wrong but it represents only a limited part of the spectrum of meaning and, as it happens, an inappropriate one. A more abstract approach would be to say, 'It seems to me that sexuality and creativity are important, perhaps compulsive, issues for you in some way and that they are connected with your need to make a big impact on the world and gain approval and recognition.'

Then the client can be invited to look at that statement and describe how it actually works for him. If he really is the all-out swinger that is assumed by the first delineation, he will recognize it readily. If he is the dignified pussycat who likes to retreat quietly into the limelight, he may not connect with the statement quite so readily but the opportunity is there for him to do so. The broader statement puts your eggs in all the baskets. With the more specific shot, you may end up with them on your face!

This is not the only reason for learning to think of astrological factors in as abstract a way as possible. Thinking of them abstractly also enables us to reduce them to a couple of basic logical cycles which, because they *are* logical, are easily remembered and provide a reliable framework on which to build our understanding of individual meanings.

Probably most people, whether they are self-taught or trained by one of the astrological teaching establishments, learn astrology essentially by a system of keywords, e.g. Aries is assertive and pioneering, Taurus is conservative and slow, the Sun is purpose, Venus is love, and so on.

Later on, students may extend their understanding so that they can, for example, write several hundred words of description of each of the signs. Yet this is really elaboration on the simple keyword. One thinks, say, of as many situations as possible in which Aries could display assertion and pioneering spirit and writes about them. So, whether we are dealing with the bald keywords in Margaret Hone or the pages of elaborate description in Linda Goodman, we still have the impression of the various signs and planets as essentially separate from each other. Their meanings, though consistent, seem arbitrary, as though somebody in the mists of antiquity had decided that it would be a good idea for the signs, planets and houses to mean what they do.

The keyword system has many advantages (I, for one, would probably have never learned astrology without it). By reducing the meanings of astrological factors to one or two easily remembered keywords, it enables us to get a secure foothold on the overwhelming mountain that astrology usually seems to be. Moreover, we are soon clambering about the lower slopes of this mountain with some confidence. If we learn the keywords and how to put them together, we can be interpreting charts (albeit stiltedly) within two or three months. So we can quickly see astrology in action and discover for ourselves that it works.

The problem is that the process is largely mechanical. It is as if we have been given a set of accurate printed labels that we can just stick on a chart to make sense of it. We neither reach an understanding of why the labels mean what they say they mean nor gain a sense of astrology as an organic unified structure. On top of that, the system encourages us to think in terms of some kind of concrete 'influence' coming from each planet and sign. Aries has an assertive *influence* on the character, Pisces a nebulous *influence* , Saturn a restricting *influence*, and so on.

This idea of influence is an old red herring which is a hangover from medieval ideas about the universe. It certainly does not accord with the picture of the universe that is emerging from post-relativity physics. The modern picture of the universe is more like that of the Eastern mystics in which everything is a reflection of everything else, in an endless dance of creation, maintenance and destruction of energies. In terms of this picture of the universe, it makes more sense to think of, for example, Saturn in the sky as being one manifestation among many of our experience of restriction and boundaries. According to this view, the planets, signs and houses are rather like lights on a control board — they show what's going on but they do not *create* what is going on.

The keyword system does not automatically assume a theory of celestial influence but it has strong overtones of such a theory, together with its accompanying fatalism. But the most practical failing of the keyword system is that it does not encourage us to think for ourselves or to *feel* and *experience* astrological meanings as distinct from them being merely convenient if arbitrary labels.

If we get down to the essence of the structure of astrology, we have a skeleton on which we can see the basic connections which we can flesh out, intelligently and accurately, as our own understanding of the spectrum of meanings of astrological symbols increases. For a start it helps to get completely away from the idea of 'influences'. If we think in terms of influence, we have to think of planets, houses and signs as environmental causes, like gravity, the weather or cosmic rays. It is much more useful, and leads to fewer blind alleys, to think of astrology as a language by means of which we can enlarge, clarify and communicate about our experiences of the world. Perhaps it can be compared with a computer 'language' in that it allows us to do things that would be tedious or impossible without it.

For the moment, let us take it that each sign, its ruling planet and the corresponding natural house represent the same principle operating on different levels. We have already looked at this idea briefly in Chapter 2 as part of the introduction to the chart analysis. Let us now look at it in greater detail.

Bearing in mind that the planet is always the action, like the verb in a sentence, we can say that the sign is a specific human need, the planet is what happens when the need becomes strong enough to require action, and the house is the circumstances that are created as a result of taking that action. An obvious analogy is eating. We always have a background need for food, whether we are aware of it or not. This is analogous to the sign. If we get hungry enough, we take some kind of action, usually eating. The eating (or perhaps doing ᵨ something else to suppress the appetite if we are on a diet) corresponds to the planet and the results, i.e., the circumstances of feeling satisfied, are the house.

It is fairly obvious that this example is a very limited part of the spectrum of meaning of Cancer, Moon and fourth house. We could do the same thing with any other sign, planet and house combination. We have a need for relationships (Libra). It gets to the point where we are attracted to someone (Venus) and circumstances to do with relationships (seventh house) are established. Notice that the house is not only concerned with the obvious, positive expression of the principle. If there is no food in the fridge or our friendship is rejected, we still have to deal with issues involving nurturing or relationships, though in the sense of absence of satisfaction about these things. This is quite an important point in chart interpretation. A stacked eighth house, for example, does not necessarily mean that the person will be engaged in a lot of sexual activity. He may be a celibate priest. What it does mean is that sexual energies will be an issue that is emphasized in some way in the life.

It might be as well here to emphasize that I am not saying that sign, planet and house are the same thing. Obviously they are not, any more than a generalized need for relationships is the same thing as falling in love or dealing with the tangible circumstances of an actual relationship. Nevertheless, they are manifestations of the same principle. They all come out of the same context.

Some writers would argue that in some cases the threefold correspondence is poor. Perhaps the most obvious instance is that of Capricorn, Saturn and the tenth house. As usually understood, both Capricorn and the tenth house have an ambitious, go-getting quality. Saturn, on the other hand, is characterized by delay and inertia. At first glance, it seems to have almost the opposite qualities of its corresponding sign and house and the pattern appears to break down.

The problem arises from a failure to recognize that we are entering the spectrum of meanings at slightly different levels. This tenth principle is to do with constructing a definition of oneself in social terms. This is something that takes time and the necessary recognition may be delayed, or seem delayed. If we emphasize the element of time in Saturn and the element of ambition in Capricorn and the tenth, we get a seeming incompatibility. In fact, the meanings of Capricorn and the tenth house also have elements of 'slow but sure' and effortful striving. For some reason, these elements are often lost in the way the sign and house are thought and written about.

It is much easier to fall into this trap of mismatching levels of meaning if we are conditioned by the prevalent idea that chart factors represent some kind of environmental influence. If we start from the assumption that they are parts of an internally consistent *language* a good many philosophical and practical difficulties clear up.

We can reduce the various sign/planet/house combinations to a series of twelve principles. These are twelve necessary stages of development which operate whether we apply astrological language to them or not. It is like Pythagoras' famous theorem about the sides of a right angled triangled triangle. If we call the hypotenuse, the side opposite the right angle, A and the other two sides B and C, then:

$$A = \sqrt{B + C}$$

This proposition is true whether we call the sides x, y, z or Tom, Dick and Harry, or we don't call them anything at all. To suppose that the letters A, B and C have an 'influence' which makes the three sides of the triangle behave in this way is obviously absurd. Yet we do the equivalent of this in the way we usually think about astrology and thereby create a host of seemingly intractable difficulties. So let us set aside for a moment the astrology and consider the twelve-stage cycle of development. It is not a particularly obvious one but it is clear enough once seen. As an example, let us take the growth of a child from the moment of birth to early adolescence.

First stage   The actual birth, the emergence into the world as an independent entity.
Second stage   Getting fed, clothed and housed, i.e., acquiring the basic necessities for the life impulse to thrive.
Third stage   Exploring the environment. Reacting to and evoking stimuli. Learning to walk and talk. All this is essentially acquiring skills and knowledge that further survival.
Fourth stage   Learning to say 'I'. Perceiving herself as a separate entity who possesses certain things and who behaves, and is expected by others to behave, in certain ways.
Fifth stage   Impressing her wishes on the environment. Making demands for recognition as a person.
Sixth stage   Training. Learning that she has to adjust her own self-expression to that of other people.
Seventh stage   Making friends of her own age. Discovering that other people exist in their own right, not merely as facilitators or frustrators of her own wishes.

Eighth stage   Becoming passionately involved with others. Almost identifying with a favourite friend or group of friends.

Ninth stage   Developing a sense of codes and customs, of what is and is not 'done' in the society in which she moves.

Tenth stage   Developing a sense of having a unique place in the group, learning to play a certain social role.

Eleventh stage   Willingly submitting to group ethics and being motivated by the general goals and desires of her group.

Twelfth stage   Realizing that she has to move on to a wider perspective. The awareness, vague at first, and perhaps resented, of a world beyond her familiar one.

A likely factor in stage twelve is the emergence of sexual feelings and we could trace a similar cycle relating to the development of the person as a sexual being. There will be hundreds, perhaps thousands, of such twelvefold cycles in a person's life. Some of them will be spread over long periods, as we have supposed our example to be. Some of them will be shorter. The stages of the cycle will most likely take irregular amounts of time. In our example being born is a much shorter process than learning social customs. Some cycles will be incomplete because they would take more than a lifetime; others will be aborted as enterprises are begun and dropped through lack of interest. No cycle will run as smoothly as the abstract example suggests. Nevertheless, the abstraction is there, logically consistent. Its stages can be labelled with the familiar names, Aries, Taurus, Gemini . . .

In order to absorb the meaning of astrology into our bones and pulses and not just into our heads, we need to become familiar with the twelve-stage cycle. If we know it intimately, our ability to read a chart on sight will be almost automatic. A good way of getting to know it is to look for your own examples of it. See if you can discover the twelve-cycles in the growth processes of the following activities:

1.   Learning astrology
2.   Getting married
3.   Writing a book
4.   Starting a business

This exercise will train you in the basics of astrology in a way keywords cannot and will eventually make you a much more fluent chart interpreter. When you really *know* the twelve-cycle, you will be able to dispense with keywords, useful as they are at an early stage.

When writing about the twelve principles I have at various times given them names, but I never feel particularly satisfied with attempts to name them. This, I now recognize, is because doing so tends to limit them to a certain area of the total spectrum of meaning. Nevertheless, it seems useful to have names for them and, bearing in mind that any simple labels are going to be unsatisfactory, we can concentrate the idea of the principles as follows.

The first principle is to do with the emergence of something so *Emergence* is a suitable name for it. Whatever emerges is then maintained so we can call the second principle *Maintenance*. Once the entity or enterprise has a basic foothold, it starts to explore its immediate surroundings. We can call this stage *Communication*. The fourth stage is concerned with establishing an identity in relation to the immediate environment so we can call it *Identity*. The next stage is the *Expression* of the identity. In the sixth stage the expression has to be adjusted to fit in with others so *Adjustment* will do as a name. Stage seven is essentially the discovery of *Relationship* and relationships are maintained, in stage eight, by *Sharing*. This leads to a wider exploring and the discovery of general principles of whatever is being considered in stage nine which can be called *Expansion*. In the tenth stage we have the establishment of a public image in contrast to the private identity of stage four, so the word *Establishment* is appropriate, with its particular social and political overtones. The next phase is characterized by team spirit or *Solidarity* and the last stage is the relinquishing of attachment to what has so far been achieved. It is difficult to think of a good single word. It is not so much renewal itself as the preliminary to renewal. Perhaps *Reappraisal* is as good a word as any.

For the sake of completeness, we will list the twelve principles, which we have just named, together with the corresponding signs, planets and houses.

Principle	Sign	Planet	House
Emergence	♈	♂	1
Maintenance	♉	♀	2
Communication	♊	☿	3
Identity	♋	☽	4
Expression	♌	☉	5
Adjustment	♍	☿	6
Relationship	♎	♀	7
Sharing	♏	♂(♇)	8
Expansion	♐	♃	9
Establishment	♑	♄	10

| Solidarity | ≈ | ♄ | (♅) | 11 |
| Reappraisal | ♓ | ♃ | (♆) | 12 |

The correspondence of Uranus to Aquarius and the eleventh house calls for comment. The correspondence appears to be rather poor since Aquarius and the eleventh are about teamwork and brotherhood and Uranus is noted for eccentricity and independence. This takes us into rather deep waters which are beyond the scope of this book. We may, however, question whether the three trans-Saturnian planets should be thought of as operating in the same way as the planets up to Saturn. I suggest that, although the trans-Saturnians *are* associated with the signs they are said to rule, the association is not the same as that of the old rulers. I am increasingly inclined to regard Mars, Saturn and Jupiter as the rulers of the houses with Scorpio, Aquarius and Pisces on the cusps and to treat the trans-Saturnians as something else. Except for the question of house rulership, this makes little difference in practical interpretation.

The use of the example of a growing child to illustrate the twelve-cycle no doubt reminded some readers of Shakespeare's famous allusion to the seven-cycle — Jaques speech in *As You Like It* which begins, 'All the world's a stage' and goes on to talk about the seven ages of man, showing a progression from Moon to Saturn. 'The infant, mewling and puking in his nurse's arms,' is the Moon; 'The whining schoolboy' is Mercury; 'The lover, with a woeful ballad made to his mistress' eyebrow' is Venus; 'A soldier, full of strange oaths' is Mars; 'The Justice, with fair round belly, full of wise saws and modern instances' is Jupiter; and Saturn is represented by 'the lean and slippered pantaloon'. The seventh age is described as 'mere oblivion' and does not fit into a planetary scheme. The Sun is not mentioned. We need not, however, worry about the closeness of the fit. The speech is not *meant* to be an exposition of astrology but an establishment of the character of Jaques. The interest of it, for our purposes, is that it illustrates a natural seven-cycle which can be linked with the planets. This seven-cycle can be reconciled with the sequence of signs if we take the Sun and Moon as being a pair. The Sun/Moon pair is balanced, at the end of the sequence, by Saturn as ruler of both Capricorn and Aquarius. It is easier to see diagramatically as above right.

☿   ♀   ♂   ♃
♍   ♎   ♏   ♐

☉ / ☽ { ♌
        ♋   ♅
                                             ♒ } ♄

♓   ♅   ♈   ♈
☿   ♀   ♂   ♃

The meanings of the planets also make up the same logical cycle but seen from a different perspective. It is not the history of something which emerges into being and grows to a natural end. It is a description of the effect on the world of a being already established in basic identity and self-expressive power. It is actually a six-cycle, not the seven-cycle that Shakespeare wrote about. Or, rather, it is a six-cycle with a pause so it is a matter of taste whether we call it a six-cycle or a seven-cycle. For the sake of consistency, we will call it a seven-cycle, since the idea of the seven is a familiar one.

The twelve-cycle and the seven-cycle sum up almost the whole of astrology. If you know them, you really know the bones of the subject. (There is also an eight-cycle — that of planetary phases — and we will discuss it in a later chapter. It has, however, a more specialized application than the other two.)

We can think of the sequence of the planets as being stages of manifestation of the will of an individual. That may sound rather grand but it can be related to quite ordinary activities, as we shall see. First of all, though, to reduce it to a logical sequence, we need to consider the Sun and Moon as being a system on its own. Not only does this make sense of the sequence of signs and rulers but it also makes sense when we come to look at the planets in terms of recognizable human activity. Astronomically, too, it is justified. The Sun and Moon are not planets and the Moon has a special relationship with the earth that the planets do not have.

The Sun, as we have already seen, is the central purpose or will to live. It is essentially a powerhouse and the characteristic of a powerhouse is that its energy is not specifically directed to any one thing. The Moon is the matrix of habits, desires, physical body, etc. that receives the solar power and brings it down to earth. A useful analogy is that the Sun is a battery and the Moon a transistor radio. By themselves, each is useless. Put them together and we have something that works.

This Sun / Moon combination is operating all the time, even when we are asleep. It is the kind of basic background of life that we have in common with the other animals. The ability to use the functions described by the planets may be what distinguishes man. Presumably all animals can perceive and biologically react to the Sun and Moon in the sky. Studies seem to show that some biological rhythms may be directly linked with the Moon in even such lowly forms of life as oysters. However, no animal has the attention span and powers of discrimination necessary to recognize the planets against the background of stars and to be aware of their motions (at least, it seems highly unlikely). So the Sun/Moon level of consciousness is what we may call instinctive. It can be very rich and complex but there is little outlet in it for the expression of personal will. The channel for personal will is represented by the planets Mercury to Saturn. The planets beyond Saturn are not connected with *personal* will.

No act of will can be accomplished unless it is first conceived and imaged mentally. Mercury, the first planet out from the Sun, is the ability to give form to creative intention. It tends to be treated in most astrological texts as a rather colourless planet but it is very powerful. None of the rest of the sequence could happen without it.

An idea by itself is not very substantial. It needs to be given value, energy, excitement. This is Venus, the second stage of the process and the second planet out from the Sun. The next stage is to take some definite action that makes an impact, however small, on the existing environment. This is Mars, the third planet from the Sun and the first one outside the earth's orbit.

What happens next is a hiatus. There is a pause, which might be a fraction of a second or might be months or years, before we can fully recognize and assimilate the results of our action. This hiatus is represented by the asteroid belt.

We cannot represent the asteroids on the chart (there are some two thousand of them) and there is no need to. As far as this way of looking at the planets is concerned, they represent a pause in the activity.[4]

---

[4] Some astrologers do use individual asteroids in interpretation and they appear to work. Such use of individual asteroids does not fit with the framework that we are considering and we will not pursue it further. I am not saying that this framework is the only possible one and, if you use asteroids and get useful information from them, by all means go on using them. The framework of planetary sequence that we are considering, though, is a valuable way of arriving at a deep understanding of what the planets mean. I would recommend that you leave experimenting with asteroids — and other exotic fauna, such as hypothetical planets — until you are thoroughly conversant with the meanings and operation of the conventional astrological planets.

After the pause we see the results of our actions, we assimilate them and are enlarged by them. This is Jupiter. We have passed the asteroid belt and we are no longer involved with purely personal action. We are now participating in the environment to some extent. Note that such expansion may be in the direction of negative consequences and, if our actions have been ill-conceived, they probably will be. It is quite misleading to think of Jupiter as a benevolent Santa Claus. It *may* work that way but there are no guarantees.

After the period of expansion, the results of the action gradually settle down into just being part of the way things are. This is Saturn, the end of the process. Saturn is the inertia of the way things are, which is why everything often looks so heavy and final when we are in the Saturn stage.

To make all this clear and more real, let us take a very ordinary example of the planetary sequence in action. You are walking along the street, past some shops. You are not thinking of anything in particular and the street is familiar enough not to demand much attention. This is the basic *Sun/Moon* level. As you stroll past a shop window, your eye is caught by a suit (male or female, according to reader!) You go closer to examine it and think that you would like to buy it. This is *Mercury*; your attention is aroused and focussed on something specific.

As you look at the suit, you start to admire its cut, its colour, the quality of the cloth, and you become excited by the thought of how good you would look in it. This stage is *Venus*, giving a certain substance and value to the idea.

You can get as excited as you like but if you do not do something about it nothing will change. So you go into the shop and tell the salesperson that you want to try on the suit. This is *Mars*, taking definite action that has a destabilizing effect on the environment.

Now there is a pause. It takes time for the salesperson to check if they have the suit in the right size and to get it off the rack for you to try it on. This is the stage of the *asteroids*.

We will suppose that everything is well. The suit looks as good on you as you thought it would, you buy it, and your experience of yourself is expanded by being the owner of a handsome new suit. This enlarged experience, which may persist for several wearings of the suit, is the *Jupiter* stage.

Eventually, after you have had the suit a while, the glow wears off and the garment becomes just another item in your wardrobe, useful and enjoyable enough, but no longer a source of particular pleasure. This is the *Saturn* stage, the end of the process.

Strictly speaking, there will be all kinds of sub-cycles going on within the main one but to consider them would only complicate the basically simple picture. As with the twelve-cycle, look for as many instances as you can of this planetary cycle in your own and other people's lives. The example of buying something is a very common one. Think back to something you bought recently. Relive the experience as far as you can and identify the stages of the cycle. Do not be content with just an intellectual labelling of the stages but re-experience them and notice how you felt. Keep it simple and do not get caught up in confusing sub-cycles (for example, there is a sub-cycle to do with paying the money which goes from the decision to buy, or imaging handing over the money [Mercury] to completing the financial part of the transaction [Saturn]).

From time to time stop and see if you can identify the stage of a cycle that you may be in at that moment. For example, as I am writing these words, I am in the asteroid stage of a cycle. The end of the chapter is in sight and I hope I shall soon be enjoying the Jupiterian glow of accomplishment. That is from one point of view. From the point of view of putting words on paper, I am in the Mars stage, taking action, though the change in the environment is small. Blank paper is being converted into paper with writing on it.

If you relate the planets to this ordinary sequence of events it will make them more real for you. They will be part of your experience, not just keywords which you only understand intellectually nor mysterious, remote forces. Of course, there is a level at which they *are* mysterious, remote forces. Venus is fancying a new suit or an ice cream, at one level. She is also the goddess of love who can overturn your entire life. It is a lot easier, though, to get to know her at the level of everyday experience.

Uranus, Neptune and Pluto do not belong to this sequence at all. In terms of the model of the psyche that we discussed in Chapter 4 on subpersonalities, they belong to the middle and upper unconscious. They too have a cycle but it is beyond the scope of the present book to go into it. For most purposes of practical interpretation they can be seen as intrusions upon the smooth running of the Saturn-bounded cycle.

The only planet we have not mentioned is the newcomer Chiron, discovered in 1977. It is a sort of lone asteroid that orbits between Saturn and Uranus. Chiron would seem to be a kind of channel facilitating a greater understanding at ordinary levels of Uranus, Neptune and Pluto. In the individual chart it seems to act as a goad or irritant, keeping the affairs of the house occupied and the energies of the planets aspected off-balance. The person is reluctantly compelled to do something to improve his or her lot in those areas. The American astrologer, Al H. Morrison, who has contributed so much to our understanding of Chiron, calls it 'an inconvenient benefic', or bringer of beneficial hard lessons.

It seems that Chiron orbs should be kept small, probably not more than 3°, even for conjunctions. Chiron does not appear in standard ephemerides as yet. [5] Whether or not you decide to use it regularly in your charts, you should experiment with Chiron and have some idea of how it works.

We began the chapter with the intention of looking at how to become a fluent, off-the-cuff chart interpreter. The best way is to learn the two cycles as thoroughly as possible and the interpretation will more or less take care of itself. In the next chapter, however, we will consider some specific examples of using these principles in direct chart reading.

[5] An ephemeris of Chiron can be obtained from CAO Times, Box 75, Old Chelsea Station, New York, NY 10113.

9.
EXAMPLE SESSIONS

For the first example of using the principles discussed in the last chapter, we will look at the chart of Sally. Sally was an actual client and the pieces of dialogue are taken from a transcript of the session. I do not generally make much use of the Marc Edmund Jones planetary patterns but if I see a grouping of planets as tight as this one I pay attention to it.

SALLY

(A astrologer; S Sally)

A   The first thing I want to say is that the planets are relatively tightly bunched on the left-hand side of the chart. This implies both a liability and an asset because your energies are firmly focussed on certain types of experience, certain circumstances of life. On the one hand it means you can bring to bear a tremendous amount of energy and drive. The problem is that there is some shutting off of other types of experience. With the planets all on the left, you are highly self-motivated. The way you 'should' be operating is with a lot of initiative, being out there and making it happen, being independent. I would think there is likely to be a problem with relationships because there is a certain unwillingness to be dependent. Does that make sense?

S   Oh yes. I feel that's one of the things which is very central to me and which I'm having to work on. It's easy for me to be in situations where I'm in the centre of things and I feel I'm giving a lot. But it doesn't allow me to feel my own needs.

A   There's a contradiction in terms here. You've just referred to the Leo part of yourself so we'll go straight to it. You have Venus, Mars and Ascendant in Leo (plus a couple of other things but

Date: *9 September 1953*   Time: *4.30 AM BST*   Place: *London*

Latitude: *51 N 32*   Longitude: *0 W 10*

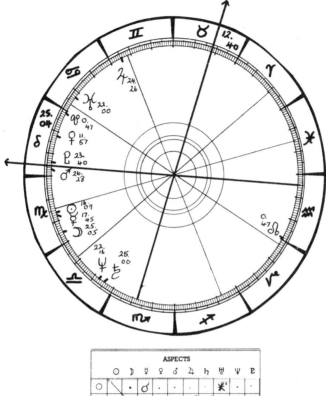

Figure 3. Sally's chart.

they're not so important for the moment). Venus is the capacity for personal love, what you like and don't like. It's the function that says 'I love you', where Mars is the function that does something about it. Mars is the more assertive. The Ascendant is the way you learn to present yourself to the world as you grow up. You learn that certain ways of being work for you; they are expected or expedient. You can call it your strategy of being in the world. With Leo rising, what you do is to be sunny (*laugh of recognition from Sally*) and open. It's a two-way thing. You also need sunny and open people around you. You need the response, the applause and the love in order to feel that you are making an impact on the world.

S   It's true. People have said that to me in other ways. I feel that people don't really see the real me because they only relate to that sunny Leo you talked about, which isn't all of me.

A   That's true. I'm not sure, though, that you're really presenting all of the sunny Leo because your Venus in Leo is also in this twelfth house section of the chart. The twelfth house is rather mysterious. At its highest, it is to do with being in touch with your own inner power. But the way in which it more often manifests is in withdrawnness and isolation. So, you've got a very contradictory pattern going on here. You've got all this wonderful Leo stuff but you don't really want to show it. And what makes it even more of a conflict is that you have Mars in Leo, conjunct the Ascendant and conjunct Pluto. That means there is a tremendous out-thrusting drive, creative, sexual, solar plexus energy screaming to be let out.

S   (*laugh of recognition*) Yes. I had a massage last night and it made me so aware of what you've just described.

A   Let's take a look at the Virgo things in your chart. You have three planets in Virgo. Virgo is best understood as a reaction to Leo. The whole idea of Leo is very much coming out onto the stage and shouting, 'Hey, folks, here I am. Everybody clap.' And sometimes they don't clap. Sometimes they throw rotten eggs. So what happens in the Virgo stage, if you get rotten eggs instead of applause, is that you learn to adjust your performance. And Virgo usually overdoes it. It goes the other way and becomes overcautious and modest and so on.

You have the Sun in Virgo. The Sun represents the central purpose of your life. Think of it as an engine that needs a certain type of fuel. So, in order to function at a really deep and central level of your life you do *need* this modesty and attitude of service to others. Virgo is essentially about service because what you are doing when you adjust your big Leo performance is that you are allowing others to have their space on the stage and their performance. So, with Sun in Virgo, you have a kind of built-in sense of discretion and appropriateness.

You also have the Moon in Virgo and that is more like where the trouble is because the Moon is the drive to create a safe support system for ourselves, the drive to fix things so that we feel comfortable, feel good about ourselves. With the Moon in Virgo, there is a tendency, whenever you feel threatened, to get into being excessively self-critical, humble and cautious.

We can see now that there is a conflict between having the very flamboyant energy and yet having to reconcile this energy with the modesty and self-criticism and service to others.

A What I think I'm hearing from you is that personal needs are not OK.

S Yes, if I'm honest, it is hard for me to admit that I *do* need certain things.

A You see, this chart is not all that universally orientated. It's not what I'd call an obvious cosmic chart, if there is such a thing. All your planets, all your engines, need very personal things in order to function. Particularly looking at Mars, which is the drive to get up and do things, for that to function you need a great deal of feedback, love, support, sex . . . you name it. The whole Leo function needs that intensely personal contact. The Virgo also needs people. Virgo can, up to a point, go along without much appreciation because he tends to feel he doesn't deserve appreciation. But Virgo still needs to see tangible results. One of the things I think is there is your having a need for all these warm goodies but with the feeling that you don't actually deserve them and shouldn't try to get them. Does that make sense?

S Yes, and I think it's something that's been on my mind quite a lot lately. Recently I have been getting a lot of positive feedback. And I've been feeling that it can't really have anything to do with me and not wanting to let myself think that it's really mine.

The rest of the dialogue was concerned with the way in which Sally was using the things that we had discovered from the chart. This relatively small, though concentrated, amount of interpretation provided enough material for the actual counselling work. If it had

been appropriate to do so, I could have gone on to talk about some
of the more important aspects and the signs on the house cusps in
much the same way as if I had been doing a written report.

This chart is a fairly easy one to deal with off-the-cuff, because
it is all clustered round the basic Leo/Virgo emphasis. Once we have
dealt with the Leo/Virgo, we have dealt with as much information
as a client is likely to be able to assimilate in one session.

GEORGE

The next chart, that of George, is very different in pattern, though
it also happens to have Leo rising. Here, the planets are just about
as widely spaced as it is possible for them to be. This may mean a
scattering of energies though, in fact, George is an ambitious, highly-
concentrated person. Although the two charts are of about the same
vintage, in George's case the Leo Pluto is in the first house. We might
expect to experience a greater degree of personal thrust and power
in his presence than with Sally and this was so.

Again, I will reproduce part of the dialogue. In both cases, I began
by talking about the structure of the chart, saying what the signs,
planets and houses were and what they represented. Whether or not
to use astrological terminology in the session is to some extent a matter
of taste. I am now inclined not to use it. The advantage of using it
is that while you are still developing the ability to sight-read charts,
it gives you something familiar to work with and focus on. The
disadvantage is that unless the client is already moderately familiar
with astrological terms, it is yet more information that he has to
contend with and assimilate. I have chosen to use examples where
astrological terms were used because they make my own reasoning
obvious. If you do use the terminology, make sure you explain it to
the client first.

A   Let's start with the first house, which is your goal and experience
    of just coming out at the world in a spontaneous, uncomplicated,
    unqualified way. The need involved here is Leo and the basic
    need of Leo is total self-expression, total self-dramatization with
    a lot of feedback. In practice it means that for you to get out
    there and do your thing, you need to be able to do it in a creative,
    dramatic way — in a big way, somehow. Your work (as a
    photographer) is one aspect but there always needs to be a touch
    of self-dramatization in the way you put yourself across.

Date: *3 January 1955*   Time: *6.55 PM*   Place: *London*

Latitude: *51 N 32*   Longitude: *0 W 10*

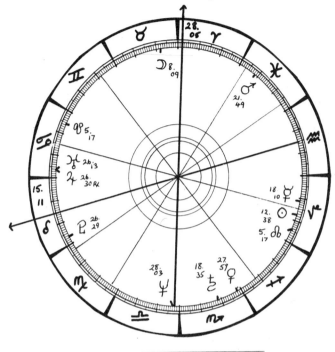

Figure 4. George's chart.

The problem that you may run up against here is that Leo wants and needs love and approval and, of course, when we come on very big and creative and dramatic we don't always get love, approval and applause. If you don't get this positive reaction, it can be very disconcerting and you'll very likely withdraw. You know, the lion stalks off with his injured dignity and goes away swishing his tail to find someplace where he's more appreciated.

G That's true. I've noticed that lately, especially to do with relationships, in the last couple of months. Sometimes I do it, sometimes I don't. It depends on the situation.

A Well, this Pluto in the first house is going to modify it quite a bit. It means you have access to a lot of unconscious energy. There's a lot of power in the way you act with people that you most likely don't know about yourself. I think you should hold that in mind.

G I can see how that works in photography. I often need to get into places that I haven't got a pass for, like pop concerts. Sometimes the only way to get in to take pictures is to hassle your way in through the stage door, just keep on at them until they let you in.

A That looks a very conscious way of using that Pluto.

G It's a very pushy way.

A What you're describing is a kind of emergency situation where you *have* to draw on this terrific persistence and power to get what you want. But I'm also suggesting that, because it is mostly unconscious, you might do something similar in ordinary situations, where you aren't aware of doing it.

G I do overdo things sometimes.

A One thing that tones it down is this square of Saturn to the Ascendant, which will bring in a more cautious, hesitant attitude. It probably works out as an alternation between being very, very self-confident and then suddenly collapsing.

G That's true, especially at the moment. Everything in my life is uncertain right now. My job, my flat, my relationship with a woman. One minute I'm sure I can handle it all and it will all work out. Then, when I've got time to slow down and think about it, I feel that I'm kidding myself. Then it starts all over again.

A And both these sides are equally valid.

G But when I've got a proper flat and I've got a real base and I can give people my phone number and my address I'm going to feel a lot better.

A Yes, that's important not only in terms of an actual home but as a general psychological pattern. Let's look at the fourth house of your chart. The fourth house is the experience of creating a safe environment of habits and feelings, ways of responding to life, certain friends and so on so that you feel comfortable with yourself. Literally, the most concrete manifestation of this is a physical house. There are two things that stand out that are appropriate to what you've just said. In the first place, with Libra on the cusp, you're going to need a place that's harmonious and attractive.

G   Yes. That's why I don't like the place I've got at the moment. It's like an open plan prison.

A   The fact that the ruler of Libra, Venus, is in the fourth just makes that even more so. It is essential for you, at the concrete, physical level, to have an attractive place to live. But, taking it back to a slightly more abstract, psychological level, it's also very important for you to be able to create a situation around yourself all the time so that you feel more or less in harmony with things. This is fine but you also have Saturn in the fourth. Saturn is where we limit ourselves. It's where we feel inferior and where it's hard for us to get it together.

G   What I want is to have a flat which is definitely *mine*. I want to share it with people but I also want to be the one who is in the position to crack the whip if I had to. I wouldn't unless they did something drastic. Then I'd throw them out.

A   OK, let's look at what you're saying because it is really what I was coming up to in talking about Saturn in the fourth. The fact that you would like to be in that situation, by definition, implies that you're not.

G   (*Repeats statements about wanting it to be his flat but not being overt about having the power. Also expresses desire for situation where he can leave the place in safe hands for a few months.*)

A   That's very appropriate to your chart. Can you come up a level from the concrete thing you're saying and see it on a different, more psychological, level? You need this safe home situation but it's difficult to get it together because this is the area of life in which you especially limit yourself. There's a sense in which you don't ever really feel quite sure of your ground, no matter how well you're doing externally. You have this feeling of needing other people around you to support you.

G   I don't know if it's to support me. I suppose it is. I don't know.

A   The implication of the chart is that something that is very important to your feeling supported is good relationships.

G   I suppose I do need people around most of the time. There's a big joke that I'm always on the phone to somebody or other. I always have to be in contact with somebody.

A   Yes, and this is where one of the crunches comes that you need to resolve. I'd say that you are a much more emotionally powerful person than you are aware of being. I suggest there's a lot of very intense feeling in you that you're not really confronting and letting out because it's too scary.

G   Yes. I have to accept that. (*with a 'disowning' laugh*)

A   The thing is, you have Libra on the fourth cusp so that you will *consciously* approach creating your support system which is dependent on relationships in a fairly relaxed, undemanding way. But inside the house is Scorpio, working in a much less conscious manner (intercepted) and which is a far more intense need. So what happens is that you come on in a cool and easy way with people but underneath it is the need for power. You've described it perfectly in saying you would like to have a place where everything would be relaxed and easygoing but where you could crack the whip if it became necessary.

Again, in terms of the way we often think that every last detail of the chart has to be interpreted, there is relatively little interpretation here. What there is, however, gets down to major issues for both George and Sally. Even if I had wanted to do more straight interpretation I could not have done because they both wanted to thrash out the issues that had been raised by the information that was given. With George, in particular, I could have almost steered the conversation so that he could talk about what he wanted to talk about without actually discussing the chart at all. Once prompted, he 'speaks his chart' very clearly.

But what about the clients who do not want to say much about themselves, who expect you to do all the work and provide them with detailed information? In this case, the problem is not very different from doing a written report except that you have to look as though you know what you are doing and you cannot keep referring to your favourite set of delineations.

As ever, the main thing is to know your subject thoroughly — to know what the planets, signs and houses mean and how they are linked in the twelve-cycle and the seven-cycle so that you can take any factor in the chart at random and say something intelligent and appropriate about it.

As I suggested in Chapter 8, it is better to rely on intuition as a guide to where to start rather than have a fixed formula. Having said that, however, I often find it useful to start by saying something about the Ascendant. For one thing, the Ascendant qualities are likely to be those the client will recognize fairly readily. With this type of client, it is important to establish a rapport at the outset by giving him something that he can see to be accurate. For another thing, in these rather daunting circumstances, intuition may go on strike and you might have to start from cold. Another option is to start with the Sun, since most people know what their Sun-sign is and have some idea of its characteristics.

CHARLES

Charles was just such a client as we are considering. He was an economist, accustomed to thinking in terms of collecting information in an objective manner so as to make decisions on the basis of it and he viewed the session in much the same way. I will not, in this instance, quote from the actual session. Rather, we will use the chart as a guide to how we might go about doing a verbal interpretation.

It helps to check to see if there are any outstanding features of the chart such as a heavy concentration in one or two signs or some major aspect patterns involving the Sun and Moon. In this case, there is a 'T'-square involving a Sun/Saturn/Neptune/M.C. conjunction opposite Moon and square to Uranus. Also, there is the Mars square Jupiter, given added emphasis since Jupiter is the chart ruler. The Mercury/Pluto square needs to be noted as well because it has a particular bearing on the circumstances of the session. People with Mercury square Pluto often tend to be reserved and sceptical. They are not particularly open to learning from other people but prefer to discover things for themselves. Add that to the emotional reserve and rigidity shown by the Sun/Moon/Saturn opposition and we can see that this is not going to be an easy nut to crack. With Sun, Venus and M.C. in Libra, though, he will probably be co-operative and friendly.

As an opening, after having briefly talked about the chart and what the various factors in it mean, we could begin with the Ascendant and say, 'Let's start by looking at the way you present yourself to the world, your strategy for coping with it. This is the kind of automatic, intuitive way you have learned of going about things that works for you and that you more or less feel is expected of you. In your case, your style is to be breezy and forthright. You come on with a lot of confidence, you don't easily take "no" for an answer once you are set on something. In fact, you probably have a tendency to go for overkill and put more

Date: *22 October 1953*   Time: *11.45 AM*   Place: *Dublin*

Latitude: *53 N 20*   Longitude: *6 W 18*

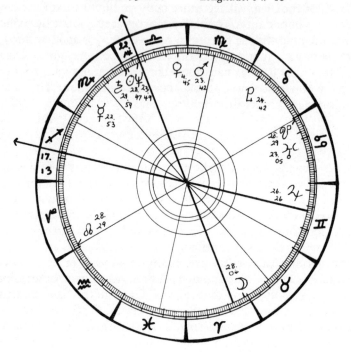

Figure 5. Charles' chart.

force and energy into things than you really need to do (Asc. □ ♂). Do you recognize yourself in that description?

Even though we may not intend to do any in-depth work, it is always worth asking the client for feedback. There are several reasons for this. One is that we want to be sure that the chart is right — or as sure as we ever can be. If Charles had denied the interpretation and said that his style was to be self-effacing and accommodating, my first reaction would have been to wonder whether there was something wrong with the birth time. As a matter of routine, I check the data with the client before we start but it is always possible that the data he believes is correct is not. The second reason is that the more work the client does, the more he gets out of the session, generally speaking. Passive listening to the astrologer is less likely to register important points than a dialogue. A third reason is that feedback keeps the astrologer going. It gives you confidence in what you are saying and helps establish a rapport. It is very daunting and exhausting to give a *bravura* performance to a client who does not say a word.

Let us suppose that in this case he says no more than, 'Yes, that's a pretty good description of me.' Where do we go next? There is not enough contact established to start touching on the difficulties implied by the 'T'-square. We could say something about the Moon in Aries — that he is restless, feels the need to be constantly in action, asserting himself, challenging the environment in order to feel inwardly secure and good about himself.

Generally the Moon is a good second point to discuss after the Ascendant but, in this case, there is the danger of getting a bit prematurely into the 'T'-square. Well, there is that stellium in Libra. It is a pretty safe bet that relationships will be of interest to him, especially as we have established that he is inclined to be over-zestful and not especially sensitive to others' feelings and reactions.

We could say something like, 'Relationships look as if they might present a few problems. They are very important to you (♎) and potentially you can get a lot out of them (♃ in 7). There are two difficulties that I can see for a start. One of them is that you would rather keep your relationships fairly light. There is a sense in which you want a lot of variety and freedom, though you have a feeling that you *ought* to be more intense and committed about them (♓ on 7; ♀ in ♏). That's OK of course, if you can find partners that will go along with it. The second thing is that there is something very uncontrollable and disruptive about relationships for you (♅ in 7). You can get suddenly turned on by someone but equally suddenly turned off, perhaps just when you don't want to be. You will react strongly against anyone wanting more than a small degree of emotional intimacy.'

Though I am looking here at ♓ on 7 and ♅ in 7, the above is, to a certain extent, true of ♎ anyway. Libra likes the *idea* of relationship but does not care so much for dealing with its realities. This is another example of the way in which important themes of the chart are usually overdetermined. They are indicated by two or three different significators.

Let us suppose that the client agrees with our interpretation and admits that relationships are not as satisfactory as he would wish. He may ask if there is anything more we can say that will throw more light on the issue. Now we come to the 'T'-square in the very sensitive angular houses. Before we actually say anything to Charles, let us consider what the 'T'-square means.

The Moon is in the fourth, which implies a great emotional sensitivity. It is in Aries, as we have seen. We can expect a lot of almost neurotic activity which Charles deliberately creates so that he never has to stop and look at how insecure he is. On top of that is the ☽ ☍ ♄ , which implies severe emotional cramping, a sense of having no access to the roots of his feelings, which are frozen below a certain level. (During the discussion, Charles referred to his feelings as 'permafrost'.)

(☉ ☍ ☽) His sense of stability, self-worth and basic right to be in the world are always at some level, possibly not conscious, in doubt. ☉ ☌ ♄ relates to a strong sense of duty, rigidity, the feeling that he is inadequate yet has to make a big effort to match up to what is expected of him. This alone will make it very difficult for him to go deeply into the issue of his feelings — he will regard doing so as self-indulgent and weak. Again, the Midheaven is involved in all this so he will set the demands of his public image and career against the needs of his poor, abused Moon.

As if that were not enough, Neptune comes into the act, sensitizing the Moon even more so that he feels entirely defenceless, yet confusing the issues so that it is almost impossible for Charles to see them properly. He probably does not even really know how badly frozen his feelings are. Finally, there is the square from Uranus, generating impatience, tension, a desire to fix it and move on, or gloss over what cannot be fixed and move on anyway.

There is material here for several years' worth of psychotherapy. We are not going to make much impact on it with a brief analysis of the situation. Nevertheless, something has to be said about it. Even a minute increase in Charles' awareness of the issues might open them up for him and increase the possibility of his doing something to resolve them. The problem is not so much *what* to say as *how* to say it. However this brings us into the realms of counselling so we will not go very far into the issue.

When discussing something as difficult as the 'T'-square, we need to have a sense of how much the person can take. If the client is obviously sensitive and depressed, we need to give the information gently. A good way to do this is by asking questions. You could say something like, 'Do you find that your feelings are squashed down a lot, perhaps because you have a strong sense of responsibility?' Then, in response to the answer, you can elaborate on what you have said and bring in the other interpretational material.

However, this chart is that of a hard-hitting, fast-moving person, something of a 'wheeler-dealer'. There is no reason why you should not give him the information quite directly. With all that fire and air, you would practically have to set a bomb off before he noticed anything anyway and pussyfooting around the issue is not likely to have much effect.

You would need to say something to Charles about the stellium in the tenth and the δ ☐ ♃. Charles is very much what you would expect of ☉, ♄ and ♆ in the tenth. He is ambitious, strongly focused on matters of career and status. The Neptune comes out in a certain tendency to cut corners and bend rules to suit himself. With all of the stellium opposing the Moon, we would expect a certain amount of career instability; the career and public image are being used to compensate for the emotional impoverishment.

The δ ☐ ♃ will tend to lead him further into the temptation that the ♆ offers. In order to gain career advantages, he will over-reach himself, take on more than he can handle and promise more than he can deliver. One should certainly tell him about this; it could well become a source of trouble.

It would be tedious to continue with every item of the chart and somewhat pointless. It is impossible to lay down rules for doing this kind of session; what I have tried to do is indicate some general guidelines.

Theoretically, it should be possible to sit down with a chart and a sheet of paper and make a list of the major themes from cold. So, with Charles, we could have made a list of the themes of career emphasis, the tendency to over-extend himself and the emotional impoverishment beforehand. I can only say that I find myself unable to do it, at least in any satisfactory way. If I have a mass of notes to work with, I can build up the themes for later presentation. If I have

the client in front of me, I can build them up as I go along. Without
either of these, I find it hard to get enough purchase on the chart
to do more than note some very general headings.

However, this may be a matter of temperament. I invite you to
try the experiment of extracting half a dozen coherent themes from
a chart, with each theme consisting of forty or fifty words as in the
Hancock and Auden charts on pages 26ff and 38-9.

10.
PHASE RELATIONSHIPS BETWEEN PLANETS

In this chapter, I want to introduce the use of phase relationships between pairs of planets. As we will see, phase relationships offer another format for organizing the chart material. They are also a source of further information which can be used with any of the formats already discussed. The reason I have not mentioned them before is that they will probably be unfamiliar to most readers and so will require a certain amount of exposition.

Phases are easy to find, easy to understand, and offer a lot of extra information for very little extra work. I use them routinely and would not think of doing a serious chart interpretation without them since they often provide a perspective that is not available from the conventional chart. Moreover, they can be reliably used when no birth time, or only a vague birth time, is available. Two of the most important phase patterns are those of Sun/Moon and Saturn/Moon. Travelling at an average of just over 13° a day, the Moon will often not move far enough in a twenty-four hour period to put the phase in doubt, as each phase is a 45° span. If it does cross the border then in cases where we have no birth time, we are left with a clear choice between two possible phases and can often determine which is the more likely by discussion with the client.

The main problem in using phases for the average astrologer is that there is not much material on them. Dane Rudhyar's book *The Lunation Cycle* deals only with the Sun/Moon phases but it describes the characteristics of the eight archetypal phases within the cycle. The tone of presentation is rather theoretical and it was Marc Robertson, in 1974, who began to develop it as a practical technique. In his book, *Cosmopsychology* Robertson extends the idea to other pairs of planets besides the Sun and Moon and gives a set of delineations. These delineations are better adapted to practical work than Rudhyar's but they still tend to be a bit too abstract. Nevertheless, I strongly

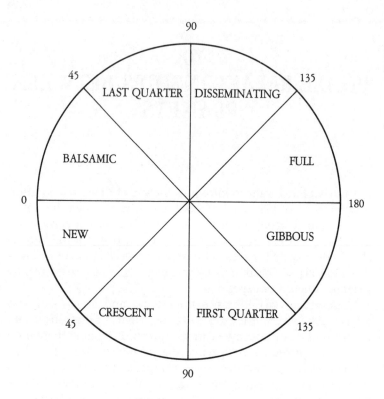

Figure 6. A phases wheel.

recommend Marc Robertson's book and also *The Spiral of Life* by 'Jinni and Joanne', which has some good material on phase relationships.

The cycle of phases is the eight-cycle referred to in Chapter 8. In Chapter 8 we saw that the twelve-cycle describes the growth of an individual being and the seven-cycle describes the process by which such a being manifests his will in the world. The eight-cycle describes the development of a relationship and the archetype of the process of relationship is that of the Sun and Moon. The cycle can be traced by the appearance of the Moon as it goes from conjunction with the Sun, through the opposition and back to the conjunction again. There are eight distinct phases, as shown in Figure 6, above. They are:

New (0-45)
Crescent (45-90)
First Quarter (90-135)
Gibbous (135-180)
Full (180-135)
Disseminating (135-90)
Last Quarter (90-45)
Balsamic (45-0)

The convention is to consider the cycle as split into the waxing half and the waning half and the phases are reckoned accordingly instead of using the 360° notation. The ideas of waxing and waning hemicycles are significant in the interpretation, as we shall see.

With three exceptions, any pair of planets can be considered in a phase relationship and so we can see how they work together even when there is no conventional aspect. The exceptions are Sun/Mercury, Sun/Venus and Venus/Mercury, which never get far enough apart to describe a cycle. In practice, attempting to consider the phase relationships of every pair of planets would swamp the astrologer with information and it is sufficient to look at five main pairs: Sun/Moon, Saturn/Moon, Jupiter/Mercury, Mars/Venus and Saturn/Jupiter. These pairs represent five basic and readily recognizable human functions, which can be described as follows:

Sun/Moon   The drive to do what one wants to do, the ability to bring energy and means together efficiently.
Saturn/Moon   The drive to conform, to do what is socially expected.
Jupiter/Mercury   The drive to communicate and expand one's share of one's environment by doing so.
Mars/Venus   The drive to express oneself as a sexual and creative being.
Saturn/Jupiter   The drive to take advantage of established structures — therefore, money-making, career.

The convention in talking about phases is to name the slower-moving planet first. The basic idea for delineating phases is that the slower planet moulds the behaviour of the faster one. A useful analogy is a radio-controlled model aeroplane. The aeroplane is like the faster planet and the radio-control operator like the slower one. The model plane has its own distinctive nature and qualities but it moves in response to the radio signals sent out by the operator.

When we consider the five main pairs of planets, it is obvious that some are going to be more personal than others as, of course, is the case with planets in signs and planets in aspect. The Saturn/Jupiter phases will each last for several months and so will describe an attitude to money that is common to a large number of people but which will be modified by the Sun/Moon and Saturn/Moon phases. The Saturn/Moon phase is likely, in most cases, to be the key one. It shows the way we conform in order to survive and the very basic imprinting that we receive from our parents. Although it is, in a sense, more superficial than the Sun/Moon phase it often dominates the latter and interferes with its expression.

The easiest way of finding phases is to use the 360° chart form as shown on page 115 and make up a dial small enough to fit it on the lines of Figure 6. All you need is a compass and a protractor. Make sure that the divisions are as close to exactly 45° each as you can make them. Cut out the diagram, mount it on a piece of light card and punch a hole in the centre so that you can line it up on the chart. It should be small enough in relation to the chart form for the planets and their degrees to be seen easily around the edge of it. There is no need to write the degrees that demarcate the phases on the dial but you can put an arrow at 0° to help with the orientation.

Let us take Maria's chart (Figure 7, page 115) as an example. First we will find the Sun/Moon phase. The Sun is the slower of the two so we centre the dial on the chart and put the zero mark against the Sun. We then look at the Moon and see that it falls clearly within the Disseminating phase. So, the Sun/Moon phase is Disseminating. Now we do the same for Saturn/Moon. We put the arrow on Saturn (the slower planet). This time the Moon falls in the First Quarter section, making the Saturn/Moon phase First Quarter. While we have the dial on Saturn, we may as well check where Jupiter is. It is in the Gibbous section so the Saturn/Jupiter phase is Gibbous. We move the arrow (or zero) to Jupiter and find that Jupiter/Mercury is Crescent. We move it to Mars and the Mars/Venus phase is seen to be Full (all this does not take much longer to do than to read about).

You may, however, prefer to use the older form of charting in which the houses are printed as equal sections. The only advantage that I can see in this method is that such a chart is rather more quickly drawn. It is a much poorer means of information display than the 360° circle, with the planets accurately located and the houses drawn in according to their proper size. However, this is a matter of taste. If you use a computer service, you will have no option but to calculate phases. As far

Date: *7 May 1950*   Time: *2.10 AM*   Place: *Belgrade*

Latitude: *44 N 50*   Longitude: *20 E 37*

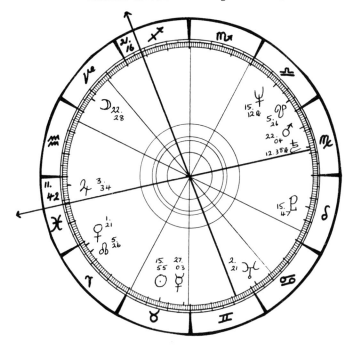

Figure 7.   Chart C (Maria).

as I know, at the time of writing, no computer service offers them. Figure
6 will enable you to do these calculations with the minimum of trouble.
First convert the positions of the planets Sun to Saturn to longitude:

Sun 45.55
Moon 292.28
Mercury 57.03
Venus 1.21
Mars 172.04
Jupiter 333.34
Saturn 162.38

In considering each pair of planets (always taking the slower as the
reference point) we first need to decide whether the phase is waxing
or waning. Is the distance between the planets less than an opposition
or not? If it is waxing, we take the longitude of the slower planet from
the longitude of the faster and locate the result in the bottom
half of the wheel. With Maria, Saturn/Moon is obviously waxing,
so we subtract Saturn from Moon:

292.28 – 162.38 = 129.54

The result is between 90 and 135 in the bottom half of the wheel
so the phase is First Quarter. The Sun/Moon phase is obviously past
the opposition and so is waning. In this case, we reverse the process
and subtract the longitude of the faster planet from that of the slower.
Since we have to subtract 292.28 from 45.55, we have to add 360
to the smaller number to make it work:

360 + 45.55 – 292.28 = 113.27

This result is between 90 and 135 in the upper half of the wheel and
the phase is therefore Disseminating. We may need to add 360 when
working with either waxing or waning phases. The calculation is a
little more fiddling than using the dial but it is still not much work
for what is potentially considerably more information. Sometimes
we need to do the calculation because the dial is not accurate enough
to discriminate between two phases when a planet is close to the cusp.
Even then, when the phase is one side or the other of a conjunction,
square or opposition aspect, we can see by eye which it is. The semi-
square and sesquiquadrate cusps need to be calculated.
    This is an important point because there do not seem to be 'orbs'

of phase (at least in terms of practical experience it works best to assume that there are not). So we treat, say, a separation of 44.59 as definitely New phase and 45.01 as definitely Crescent. In theory this means that we should interpret an applying semi-square (or square, sesqui-quadrate, opposition and conjunction) differently from a separating one. In practice, I find this an unnecessary complication. I interpret aspects in the usual way and then use the phase relationships to provide extra information.

We now know how to find phases and we have identified five pairs of planets to which it is particularly useful to apply them. We now need to discover what the phases mean so that we can use them for interpretation. As with the signs and planets, what we are really dealing with is the development of a cycle. This is a cycle which describes the interplay of two forces in a relationship. Again, it is useful to consider a concrete example in order to begin to get the feel of what the cycle means. The most obvious example to choose is that of a love relationship.

New   First meeting, spontaneous attraction. Both parties are plunged into the relationship whether they want it or not.
Crescent   The need to allow for difficulties and differences. Some conscious effort is needed to make the relationship work.
First Quarter   Making a decision and a commitment which changes the relationship, e.g. deciding to get married.
Gibbous   Dealing with the results of that decision. Discovering day-to-day techniques for living together. Making adjustments to each other.
Full   Both partners have to face up to whether the marriage is working or not. An opportunity for creating conscious unity, as opposed to the unconscious unity of the New phase.
Disseminating   The relationship is well established and working smoothly. The partners have arrived at a mode of living that they do not have to work at consciously.
Last Quarter   The purpose of the relationship begins to change and they begin to want something more from it. They may, for example, decide to have and actually conceive a child.
Balsamic   Waiting, looking to the future and the beginning of a new cycle which, this time, is to do with parenthood. The focus is on potential rather than on immediate activity.

For ease of interpretation, the phases can be reduced to keywords and they can, to some extent at least, be considered as analogous to pairs of signs. There is no theoretical justification for this but, since signs are familiar and phases are not, the similarities that exist can be utilized. The keyword meanings and (partial) sign correspondences are:

Phase	*Keywords*	*Signs*
New	Spontaneity, creation	♈ / ♌
Crescent	Effort, holding on	♏ / ♋
First Quarter	Unconsidered action	♈ / ♐
Gibbous	Adjustment, consideration	♍ / ♑
Full	Awareness, confrontation	♎ / ♊
Disseminating	Smooth running	♋ / ♉
Last Quarter	Considered action	♒ / ♑
Balsamic	Focus on potential	♏ / ♓

We need to bear in mind that phases are different from signs but it will certainly help, in interpretation, to know that, for example, a New phase Sun/Moon (or Mars/Venus or whatever) is something like having Sun and Moon simultaneously in Aries and Leo. Incidentally an important phase relationship often accounts for characteristics which are not evident from the conventional chart. We may find someone who is, say, all earth and water but who has a certain dash and fire that does not quite seem to be in the chart. Such a person might well turn out to have a New Moon in Taurus, or something of that kind.

A couple of examples of deriving meanings will enable you to construct your own meanings for each of the five pairs and eight phases. Let us take Last Quarter Sun/Moon and Disseminating Mars/Venus.

The Sun/Moon phase describes one's ability to do what one inwardly wants to do. Last Quarter phase is action, often stressful, as a result of inner change. We can bear in mind the Capricorn/Aquarius flavour of this phase and our delineation might be: 'There are feelings of inner stress and the desire to act forcefully but action is often inhibited by inner doubts. The need for action arises from inner pressure and it may well be opposed by people in the immediate environment. The Last Quarter type is often extremely frustrated. He sees dimly what desirable changes are needed but the pressures of outer circumstances and past conditioning make it difficult for him to actualize those ideals.'

The Sun/Moon phase is, of course, a very comprehensive one. If we are discussing, say, the Mars/Venus phase, we would apply the above reasoning specifically to sexual and creative energies, and so on with whatever pair of planets is being considered.

Our second example is Disseminating Mars/Venus. The Disseminating phase is smooth running; one's patterns of beliefs are lined up to support one's expression and the expression is tailored to suit the circumstances. So, there is a good deal of confidence and conviction available to the person operating in a disseminating phase. It should not, however, be supposed that this is totally desirable. One can get stuck in the smooth, confident expression of some essentially limited patterns. Applying the meaning to Mars/Venus, which is sex and creativity, we have: 'This person has clear basic beliefs about love which work smoothly for him. He knows what he wants and how to get it. He can be absolutely charming, feeling secure in his approach to love and sex and moving ahead with reassuring confidence.'

Once you have become accustomed to using phases, I suggest you use them regularly for interpretation work. For the sake of keeping the material under control, it is best to limit them to the five main pairs of planets but sometimes it is useful to look at the phase relationships between other pairs. For instance, if a client says he has difficulty in enjoying himself, we can look at the phase relationship between Saturn and Venus, especially if there is no recognized aspect between them. If he wants to talk about his ability to get results, we can look at the Jupiter/Mars pair, to see how he combines action and expansion.

Apart from this usage, the five main pairs, with their phases, can be used to structure a written or tape recorded report. They can be particularly useful when a psychological approach is required. The basic technique is to describe the pattern of each of the sections, as shown by the phase relationship, then to elaborate by describing the sign and house position of the two planets and the aspects that they are involved in. Here is a full example using Maria's chart, shown in Figure 7, page 115.

ANALYSIS OF CHART C

For the purpose of this analysis, we will consider five distinct aspects of your personality. These are:

1. The ability to go for what you want.
2. How you conform to what people expect of you.
3. How you communicate and express yourself.
4. Love, sex and general creativity.
5. Potential for career and financial success.

These categories are, of course, somewhat arbitrary and they will overlap to some extent. Nevertheless, they are useful in helping to establish a clear picture.

1 Going for What You Want

(☉ / ☽ DISS) You are able to go for what you want in a way that is relatively easy and untroubled. This does not mean that you always get what you want without difficulty. But you do have a general sense of rightness about your goals. You believe that you deserve to attain them and you do not question or doubt this very much. This is a very powerful pattern and enables you to have a considerable impact on the world.

A danger with this pattern is that you can get carried away by your own convictions of rightness and easily believe that what is right for you must also be right for other people. There may be some tendency to intolerance which, perhaps, especially shows itself in an impatience with people who are not so positive and active as you are (☉ △ ♂; ☽ △ ♂). You will be inclined to fairly high levels of energy and to believe in taking the initiative and 'grasping the nettle' in very forthright ways.

(☉ in ♉) Your general sense of what you want in life is focused on developing a sense of stability and rootedness. Probably material possessions will be important to you. At any rate, you need to have situations in your life that feel solid and that you can rely on. It is important for you that you should quickly be able to see tangible results for your efforts. You will be inclined to appreciate the physical things of life and you will basically be practical and down to earth. This goes with a markedly conservative streak. Once you have settled on some way of doing things you will be reluctant to change it, even when it needs to be changed because it is no longer working. You have strong feelings under what is, perhaps, a placid exterior and sometimes your reluctance to change is caused by a sentimental attachment to old ways (☉ ∟ ♀). Some of it is a fear of change; you are possibly overconcerned with issues of security and maybe inadequacy (☉ △♄). The positive side of this is a considerable capacity for endurance and self-discipline. All the same, you have an urge to break out and do something different (☉ ⊼ ♆). The conflict between these two forces may well produce a good deal of tension and you will be inclined to deal with it by escaping from it in various ways and perhaps pretending that it is not really there. The ways of escaping may be anything that blurs the edges of reality a little, daydreaming, TV addiction, maybe smoking or tranquillizers. A lot of the tension comes from the fact that you have a powerful drive for success and achievement which you probably do not fully recognize (☉ □ ♇). You do, however, have a kind of sunny openness about the way you present yourself to people which very likely gets you a lot of what you want without your having to make much conscious effort about it (☉ * Asc.). You do, though, have to make a conscious effort to show your 'best side' to the greatest advantage.

That deals with what you want. Now, there is a kind of set of assumptions that we have about ourselves and about life that enables us to make what we want a reality. Sometimes the two things can be at odds but, in your case, they are not. They work together very smoothly. It is true that your basic assumptions about life are centred around the proposition that you will always have to work hard to get what you want (☽ in ♑). You do not mind that, though. You have plenty of ideas and plans that keep you going (☽ △ ♂; ☽ △ ☿). A problem here is that you may be so much concerned with the idea of having to work for what you want that if you get something without much effort you may feel guilty. You may feel as though you have cheated in some way and not be able to enjoy it as much as you deserve. As we have seen, you probably are rather 'lucky', so this may be a difficulty that you will need to pay some attention to, if you are to make the most of your opportunities and good fortune.

Generally speaking, though, in almost all respects your ability to go for what you want is very functional and, in broad terms, you should be reasonably successful in life without very much effort. There are certain areas which do present some difficulty, notably that of love and sex, which we will look at later.

2 How You Conform to What Others Expect

As we grow up we all learn that we are expected to be a certain way. We get 'messages' from our parents or other adults who are around when we are children that, in effect, tell us what we have to do and how we have to be in order to make it with them and get their approval — which, of course, is essential to us when we are very small. This kind of patterning to a large extent makes up the battery of basic assumptions about life that we mentioned in the last section. Sometimes, what we have to do to conform is very much at odds with what we inwardly want.

In your case, the two do not drastically oppose each other but they are not particularly harmonious either. As we have seen, the natural way you go for what you want is relatively easy going. You expect to have to work hard but you also expect a fairly ready recognition and reward for your work.

At the level of what is expected of you, though, you are much more forceful ($\hbar$ / ☽ 1st Q). You are perhaps not very clear what *is* expected of you but you feel obliged to be seen to be putting a lot of zest and energy into it. In other words, you feel that you are supposed to act rather tough and aggressive while your deeper nature is much milder. Obviously, there can be conflict here and you may sometimes become exhausted because you feel unaccountably obliged to be brisk, efficient and assertive while inwardly you do not feel that way.

One area in which you may especially feel that you have to be brittle and aggressive is in relationships ($\hbar$ in 7). Probably what often fuels or provokes your aggression is the sense that other people are not coming up to your standards and expectations. You can be very demanding and critical and some of this has its roots in a fear of chaos ($\hbar$ ℞ in ♍). At some level of your mind you may fear that things will get completely out of hand if you do not keep a tight rein on them. So, when other people are sloppy or do not keep appointments on time or do what they say they will do, it provokes you beyond what is actually necessary and you over-react. Remember that what we are talking about is a kind of 'survival programming' which dates back to infancy and which you are most likely not even conscious of now.

Although you have this forceful quality, there is a curious sort of defensiveness that goes with it ($\hbar$ ☍ Asc.). You might well reconcile the two by having a slightly excessive sense of propriety and dignity which is not always appropriate to the situation. Because of this, you may also find that it is not always easy to say what you want to say and are likely to feel misunderstood to some extent ($\hbar$ ⊼ ♆). This, again, may provoke an aggressive and/or over-dignified response in you. So, it can be a vicious circle. Again, there is a certain amount of escapism and avoidance of being clear about what is going on. Your general sense of what other people expect of you is probably quite badly confused and it would repay some thought on your part (☽ □ ♆).

3 How You Communicate and Express Yourself
This section deals with your ability to communicate with others by expressing what you know and believe. This is important for your emotional health because, on a slightly deeper level, it refers to your skill at coping with and influencing your environment.

The basic feeling about it for you is that it is hard work. There is a sense of struggle about getting yourself across (♃ / ☿ CRESCENT). In all probability what happens in practice is that you tend to overdo it to compensate for your own feeling that you are not having as much effect as you wish. Sometimes the sense of the effort you have to make interferes with your perception of what is appropriate. When you are struggling to get your views across, other people may experience you as being insensitive to what they see as the real issues or they may experience you as being over-emphatic (☿ □ ♃). You are inclined to be self-conscious and often feel as though you are putting on an act. You need to simply allow yourself to be aware of this and to learn to trust that your message will get over without forcing it, in spite of how it may seem to you.

This act of communicating consists of two factors. One is your sum total of beliefs and knowledge which also contains your need to assimilate and influence your environment. The other is the verbal and mental skill with which you express this. These factors can be considered separately.

Your sense of what you know and your desire to expand into your environment is inclined to be very emotional and not particularly clear (♃ in ♓). It is characterized by a basic sincerity and kindliness which will come across despite your often over-strained attempts to express it. It is easy for people to appeal to your sympathies and you may feel guilty unless you help them, whether or not they really need or deserve your help. You are capable of a great deal of self-understanding and you need to find time to be alone now and again (♃ in 12). This is because you find your resources much more within yourself than in your contacts with other people. Also, your over-ready sympathies may lay you open to being drained by other people's demands. This is especially true since you tend to project this quality of sympathy and vulnerability fairly obviously (♃ ☌ ♓ Asc.). There is a limit to this, though, and you have a built-in ability to see clearly what is going on in a given situation and react forcefully against it, if need be (♃ △ ♅). Obviously, this adds a note of clarity and realism to what might otherwise be too much sympathy and even gullibility.

The second factor, your ability to use verbal and mental skills, is rather different (☿ in ♉). There is still an emotional, intuitive quality about it but it is much more practical and down to earth. The first impression people are likely to get when you talk to them is that of shrewd commonsense. Your style of thinking is likely to be methodical and slow, possibly inclined to run in familiar grooves so that it is difficult for you to see new angles and points of view. In fact, when your sympathies are *not* engaged, you may be quite difficult to argue with because you persist in going over the same ground again and again and are not easily convinced. There is often considerable force and edge to what you say and a certain restlessness about you (☿ △ ♂). This sharpness has to contend with a desire to be agreeable and charming (☿ ✴ ♀). The pattern in you is such that you probably blend these conflicting factors very harmoniously. You are able to say what you think in a direct manner but with so much charm that it does not sting or give offence. A difficulty that may crop up is that you are not always clear enough about what you are trying to say (☿ ▢ ♆). You may tend to take too much of a listener's knowledge for granted, making it difficult for him to follow you.

4 Love and Sex

This heading needs little explanation and the two factors involved are perhaps a bit more obvious than with the other sections. Briefly, they are your capacity to attract others and be attracted to them, and your ability to do something about it. They could also be described as what you want and what you go for. The two things can be very different.

In your case, they are indeed likely to be very different (♂ / ♀ FULL). Your love life is likely to be romantic and dramatic because in many ways it seems to you to be a challenge. It is as though you do not know what you want from a love relationship and you keep plunging into challenging situations in an attempt to find out. This does not necessarily mean that you will be involved with a lot of different men, though it may. It could just as easily mean that your love life is focussed on one person but there will be something dramatic about the circumstances of that relationship. Part of what is needed here is for you to become more reflective and conscious about what you expect from love. It is as though the ideas about it that you picked up early in life, probably from your parents, do not work for you in practice at all. You need to form your own ideas from experience and there is a certain amount of desperation in it so you do it the hard way. What is really going on in a relationship is that you are trying to balance out and overcome a deep division within yourself. You are very prone to see qualities in another person, whether these qualities are good or bad, that are really your own but which you are unaware of or not very clearly aware of. We all do this, of course, but for a person of your love-type, it is an issue that particularly needs to be confronted. When it is confronted, you are capable of conscious and fulfilling relationships. To the extent that you rely on your feelings only, you create difficulties. Often, you create a misleading impression of what you want and so feel misunderstood yourself.

Matters are not made easier by the fact that your capacity to attract others and be attracted by them operates in a way which is impulsive, urgent and often idealistic (♀ in ♈ and 1). At some level, when you are strongly attracted to someone you feel that person is absolutely essential to you. It might not be as conscious as that but the feeling is so powerful that you are not really very sensitive to what the other person wants (♀ ⊡ ♇). At the bottom of it there is a kind of demand that he *must* love you because you want it so much. You may not be able to articulate this. In fact, it is possible that sexual feelings are so strong that you automatically block them to some extent and you can find yourself being inappropriately formal and rigid in your attitudes. You can be very easily turned on in a way that is probably disconcerting because of the depth of feeling it reveals. As a self-protective mechanism you may have learned to turn off quickly as well. That is another mechanism that is not now entirely within your conscious control and you may find it operating when you least want it to. One effect of this is that you may frequently find yourself acting in a casual, flirtatious, uncommitted way which is very far from how you actually feel. Pride is likely to play a big part in determining your behaviour in a love relationship. In fact, the essence of your difficulties may be that you would ultimately rather keep your pride intact than have love (♀ ☐ ♅).

As to what you do about being attracted to someone, there is again rather a contrast. Your feelings are something of a volcano but your mode of putting them into action is quite cautious and even fussy (♂ in ♍). In fact you can be so fussy that hardly anyone appeals to you sexually in the first place. This kind of uncertainty about your own physical response adds to the problems you have with your volcanic feelings — you do not find much that gives them an outlet. So, when you do meet someone who excites you physically, you are likely to be very faithful to him, even subservient to the extent of ordering your life the way *he* wants it to be, no matter how unreasonable or inconvenient. If this sounds inconsistent with what we have just seen about pride, it is! You are capable of holding both of these two totally inconsistent attitudes. Some of the way you reconcile the two is by telling yourself that you do the things you are doing in order to improve your partner and induce him to come up to scratch in the ways in which he inevitably falls short. Your tendency to be critical of your partner will be enhanced by the feeling, vague or otherwise, that your choice of partner and your sexual behaviour generally reflects on your public image, perhaps on career prospects (♂ ☐ M.C.). So, as well as having your own exacting standards, you will worry about what the neighbours think.

5 Potential for Career and Financial Success

The two factors that are involved in this section are ones that we have looked at before. The first is what you know and believe and your desire to expand into and influence your environment. The second is your perception of what limits you and restricts you or even entirely prevents you from expanding. Much of this restriction will appear to be the way the world is and the expectations it has of you to fit in with that way.

In you, the two factors operate together so that there is a certain lack of self-confidence ($\hbar$ / $\mathcal{4}$ GIBB). It helps a lot if you can plan ahead of time and be highly organized in anything to do with your job or money. Relying on instinct and intuition in these areas does not really work for you. You need a solid and proven way of doing things that you have learned from your own personal experience. This is a matter of learning by trial and error and beginning in a small way. As far as career goes, you are probably happiest in a job where your abilities are not stretched too much and your responsibilities are clearly defined. At least, this is so until you find your feet. As your confidence grows in your ability to actually do the job you can raise your sights and look for promotion. Do not try to land some job that is beyond your current capacities and hope that you will grow into it. Some people can operate very successfully that way but you are not one of them. You would find the strain on your confidence very wearing and feel yourself to be a fraud, even though you might be performing quite well. There is a perfectionist streak in you and you do not allow yourself to get away with things. A danger of this, of course, is that you will be *too* exacting with yourself and not realize that your level of competence in a job has risen. So it is likely that you may currently be operating at a level below your capacity and earning less than you could be.

This uncertainty extends to the way you handle money. The desire to save and the desire to spend clash in a rather irritating way and you need to keep some kind of balance. It is best for you to keep a constant check on your income and expenses, even if you happen to have plenty of money. Having your financial affairs in a condition where you can balance your cheque book at a few minutes notice will relieve your life of unnecessary strain.

11.
MAKING IT REAL FOR
THE CLIENT

We have seen that the essence of synthesis is the assimilation of the information by the client. This is not at all the same thing as simply acquiring it. A client can *acquire* a great deal of information about himself in a single session. He may recognize it and assent to it but, at that level, it makes very little difference to him and he will forget most of it in a few days under the pressure of day-to-day living. There is little or nothing to be done about this in written or tape recorded work. All we can do is make the best possible job of analysing and organizing the material and hope that the client will be motivated to apply what he learns which in most cases, unfortunately, probably will not happen. However, as I said in discussing Charles' chart, even a minute increase in self-awareness will eventually bear some fruit. It is by no means unknown for a client to be helped by something in a written analysis five, or even ten, years after it was done.

Synthesis, then, consists of the client making the information real for himself, in turning the bald data into living experience. To some extent this will happen spontaneously but it is not likely to happen to any great extent. It stands a better chance of happening if the interview is structured to facilitate it. In practice this means that the client needs to be engaged in a *discussion* about the chart. Most consulting astrologers tend to think solely in terms of *telling* the client about himself. They would treat an interview more or less as a face-to-face version of a written or recorded report and deliver the information without much concern for the effect it is having on the client.

Some clients like this approach. They do not want to reveal very much of themselves and resent any attempts to get them to do so. In such cases, the purely information-giving approach is adequate and appropriate. What is not so adequate and appropriate is that many astrologers shrink from confronting the psychological reality of the client's problems — and their own. They prefer to remain with a cerebral and abstract interpretation which is handed out with little sense of how relevant it may be to the client's actual needs. They use the chart in a detached and impersonal way and would be horrified if anything 'human and messy', as a psychotherapist of my acquaintance put it, should happen.

In the last five or ten years, a new trend in astrological *counselling* has been emerging. Astrologers of this persuasion are less concerned with giving detailed information and more concerned with using the information to open up a client's awareness. This means abandoning the doctor/patient model of counselling and instead considering the discussion as an interaction between two equals one of whom, the astrologer, has access to some specialized information.

To complete the discussion of chart synthesis, it is necessary to say something about the issues involved in counselling, though at the risk of going beyond the scope of this book.[6] Perhaps the most important thing is to have some sense of the dynamic forces of the psyche. There is a strong tendency among many astrologers to talk as if everything were within the clients' conscious control and that they merely need to be given appropriate advice and information. This can lead to such futilities as telling a Virgo Moon to 'Try not to worry'. More sensibly, however, it can still mean that clients are given advice and information which, though positive and accurate, they are quite unable to apply.

A good example is Charles again. The obvious thing to say to Charles, with his stacked tenth house and Mars square Jupiter, is, 'Whatever you do, curb your tendency to over-reach yourself or you will be in trouble'. As Charles was not willing to do any in-depth work during the session I could do little more than point out the tendency to him and suggest that he keep an eye on it. He recognized the tendency readily enough and had no difficulty in seeing that it could lead him into trouble and had, indeed, led him into trouble in the past. Yet the very next time the opportunity arose, he over-reached himself in a way that could have damaged his credibility with his employers and which resulted in strain that brought about a major breakdown in his health. Whatever intellectual awareness he retained from the session was swept away by much more powerful forces beyond his control.

[6] For more detailed information see Christina Rose *Astrological Counselling*, Wellingborough: Aquarian Press (1982); and Roy Alexander *The Astrology of Choice*, York Beach: Samuel Weiser (1983).

So much for astrology! Any consulting astrologer can tell similar stories of sound advice given, but not taken, with disastrous results. Thus, we might tell a client with a severely afflicted Neptune in the seventh not to get involved in any kind of business partnerships. He himself sees the sense of it, knowing from past experience that he is too gullible. Yet along comes what looks like the opportunity of a lifetime and he plunges in. Before he knows what has happened, his partner is off to South America with the money on the next plane!

Experiences like this can be very disheartening to the astrologer (to say nothing of the client) but today there is really no excuse for the kind of psychological naivety that engenders them. Twenty or thirty years ago, when much of the current astrological thinking and practice was being developed, it was difficult to learn much basic psychology. The theories of Freud and Jung seemed elaborate, complicated and scarcely relevant to practical astrological consulting. Most astrologers were inclined to feel that unless they were in a position to train as Freudian or Jungian analysts, they should not get involved with psychology. In the sense that a little learning is a dangerous thing, this was no doubt a wise move. In practice, it has led to the situation described above, where unconscious factors are ignored in the vague hope that they do not apply or will go away, and the client is treated as though he can control what happens.

Now the situation has changed. Though astrologers should be clear that they are not therapists, they can learn much from the various forms of humanistic therapies that have developed since the early 1960s and apply it in their astrological sessions.

One thing that is much clearer than it was twenty or thirty years ago is that we unconsciously run our lives on the basis of decisions about the world that we make as very small children. These decisions are made in response to what seem to the child to be circumstances that threaten his very survival. Recent work suggests that a baby has a much higher degree of intelligence and consciousness right from birth, and even in the womb, than was previously thought. If this is so, then every child experiences some pretty cruel treatment. They may be hauled into the world with metal forceps, from darkness into glaring lights, possibly half doped with drugs from the mother's bloodstream, then held upside down, slapped and, as soon as possible, bundled off into a cot and left to cry their hearts out. All this is justified because babies are not supposed to know any better. If, as now seems likely, babies *do* know better, it is no wonder that none of us remember our early childhood.

The baby will not be able to put it in so many words but, after a few days of this kind of treatment, he is going to get the idea that the world is a hostile place and that he is helpless in the face of this hostility. This means that a person builds his life around a core of fear, pain and anxiety. Much of our subsequent behaviour, including most of what we think is rational and realistic, consists of strategems for coping with, or avoiding, the basic fear, pain and anxiety.

According to the psychoanalyst Karen Horney,[7] there are three basic strategies. She calls them 'moving against', 'moving towards' and 'moving away from'. These result in deeply entrenched patterns of living in which we seek to master people and circumstances; seek to propitiate them and efface ourselves or seek to remain aloof and uninvolved. In the first instance, the person is constantly active and striving, a fighter who regards people as adversaries and challenges. In the second case, the person is modest and accommodating, anxious to adapt himself to others' needs. In the third case, the person often seems stronger and more balanced than the other two. He has a certain integrity that comes from a powerful desire to avoid both warm contact and friction with others. Basically he does not want to be bothered with anything and avoids any kind of change.

I have listed the three types in the order in which Karen Horney enumerates them. Reverse the order of the last two and they clearly relate to the astrological qualities cardinal, fixed and mutable. Unfortunately, the chart does not seem to indicate the type in any very obvious or simple way. Charles was clearly the first type, the fighter, and there is, of course, a heavy emphasis on cardinal signs in his chart but the correlation is not usually as obvious as that.

So, we have an unconscious mechanism which is powered by basic pain, anxiety and fear. On top of that is a generalized pattern of response which is usually predominantly one of the three types (there are, of course, always traces of the other two). On top of that again there are the specific ways of thinking, feeling and acting that result from the kind of psychic atmosphere created by the parents.

Though it is unconscious this mechanism can be, and is, constantly reactivated by the things that happen to us and even merely by people and objects that are just passively there. It is like the mechanism of a juke box that will always select and play the same record when a particular button is pushed. To stay with the example of Charles, he is, as we have seen, a fighter. He sees the world in terms of winning

[7] Karen Horney. *Neurosis and Human Growth*, New York: W. W. Norton (1950).

and losing, outwitting others or being outwitted. There is also something specific that he picked up from his parents (probably, with his Moon in Aries, his mother) that always says to him, 'Chance it. Take a risk.' There is an unconscious compulsion to wheel and deal and to put himself on the line with too few resources.

When the right button is pushed that is what he will do, regardless of what he knows intellectually about the dangers of over-reaching himself. He is unable to act in his own intelligent best interests where this particular issue is concerned. It would be unrealistic to imagine that his being told about the pattern by an astrologer is going to have any effect on this unconscious mechanism which is literally concerned with life or death.

Charles has no interest in examining his motives and so, in a session, there is no possibility of getting him to look at the mechanism and so become more conscious of how it works. (Becoming conscious of, and disidentifying from, the mechanism weakens it and enables a person gradually to break the grip of such a pattern.) In terms of the theory of subpersonalities, this Mars square Jupiter in Charles' chart is a kind of 'Gambler' subpersonality, always ready to put his shirt on an outside chance and, quite frequently, lose it. We can only hope that, when he has lost his shirt often enough, he will begin to be motivated to look at himself in some depth. (I am not, of course, suggesting that everyone with Mars square Jupiter will have a 'Gambler' subpersonality. In Charles' case it is emphasized by the heavily-loaded tenth house and the need to be publicly successful to compensate for emotional insecurity.)

Charles is willing to know *about* and to talk *about* his tendency to over-reach himself and his frozen emotions. He is at least receptive to information on those issues. He is *not* willing to experience the issues directly. Probably there is panic and fear of losing out at the root of the rash and over-reaching behaviour. (Fear and panic, Phobos and Deimos, are the Martian satellites.) I say 'probably' because we were not able to discuss the problem in enough depth to find out. If he truly allowed himself to experience that fear and panic instead of rushing into action, he would be afraid of being overwhelmed by it. He is being run by a process which goes something like: fear of losing out provokes excessive risk-taking, which usually damages him in some way — and so he loses out. He is not aware of this process, only of the effects of it.

This illustration applies to all of us. Our lives are full of these processes which continue with full force, despite our conscious resolutions about them, *because* we do not allow ourselves to experience them.

Paradoxically, the way to disidentify from something is first to accept it and *experience* it, without making judgements about it.

Simply acknowledging the truth about our lives works. If we have never actually done it, that statement may sound very improbable. But, remember, I am talking about really *experiencing* something, not just having an *intellectual* concept of it. It is not enough to say, 'I have a tendency to over-reach myself' or 'I have a problem feeling close to anyone', or whatever. That is a necessary first step and one that astrology can help with. But to actually change things we have to experience the feelings and body sensations that are part of the issue and be willing for them just to be there.

It is not easy and astrologers, by the very nature of their craft, have an extra avoidance mechanism, i.e., they focus on the chart, the interpretation, the astrological *explanation* of the problem instead of being with the problem itself. Part of the tendency to talk as if everything were under the client's control is the hidden assumption that labelling something makes a difference to it. A lot of astrologers, especially beginners, on hearing that someone has difficulty with emotional closeness, will say, 'Ah, you've got Moon opposite Saturn' as though that disposed of the matter. In a great deal of astrological writing and teaching there is an implicit assumption that if we can relate a client's difficulty (or our own) to some chart configuration, it somehow shifts the whole thing onto a more lofty plane.

Nobody says that in as many words, of course, but there are many books on interpretation, excellent in themselves, that avoid the question of what interpretation is *for* and leave the distinct impression that it has no other end but itself. In a way, this is understandable. Learning to interpret a chart is difficult enough and requires fairly undivided attention over a period of three or four years. It is natural that the first concern of both teachers and students should be for the students to learn to interpret accurately and fluently. The result, unfortunately, is that very little attention has been given to the effective use of the information thus gathered.

The situation at the time of writing is that astrology has been developed into a powerful diagnostic tool which is capable of providing profound insights. A few astrologers are beginning to tackle the issue of effective application of the diagnosis and seeking to develop a technology of using the chart information as productive as the technology we already have for extracting it.

The principles of such a technology are at once simple and difficult. They are simple because they boil down to nothing more than bringing ourselves, or our client, to tell the truth about what is actually so. They are difficult because we all have an enormous resistance to doing this, a resistance which stems from the entire unconscious mechanism that is set up in childhood to deal with the pain, fear and anxiety.

Furthermore, there is a major difference between the two technologies. The technology of extracting the information — chart interpretation — works quite well at a purely intellectual level. It works a lot better if we experience the truth of astrological symbolism at deeper levels but we can do a fair job with a purely cerebral grasp of the meanings. Even a computer can do it! The technology of using the information for personal change, however, does *not* work in terms of head knowledge. *It is completely different from interpretation.* It is hardly possible to emphasize that statement too much or say it too often. Failure to realize the difference is what keeps the practice of astrology at a rather low level of effectiveness.

Unless you are already familiar with the material I am going to discuss now, it is going to do strange things to your head! In Chapter 1 I said that astrology is weird — a fact which we tend to avoid confronting. You may have considerable difficulty in understanding what I am saying simply because it is outside the familiar framework within which we think and perceive. It may help if I describe briefly the work that has been done recently on the functions of the right and left hemispheres of the brain. The left hemisphere is to do with logical thinking and is the most favoured in our culture. It operates by manipulating ideas and things rather than by experiencing directly. It knows how to use words and to put things together in order. The right side of the brain is non-rational. It grasps things as wholes, as they are, without judgements — it is intuitive and does not need a basis of reason or facts in order to function. It operates in terms of poetry rather than logic. Generally speaking, we do not use it very much.

The difficulty that you, the reader, are almost certainly experiencing is because having spent almost the entire book so far dealing with familiar left hemisphere material, I have now switched over to material which is the province of the right hemisphere. What makes matters worse is that I have to use left hemisphere techniques — words — to attempt to convey it. This means that your brain's left hemisphere will think it should be able to understand the material in the usual way and will be uncomfortable when it cannot.

Just to illustrate briefly the difference in perception between the two halves of the brain, consider this famous line from Othello: 'Keep up your bright swords, for the dew will rust them.' The line can be paraphrased accurately as 'Your swords will get rusty if you're not careful.' Both original and paraphrase can carry the overtone of slightly contemptuous command that is implicit in the context of the line. This is all left-brain stuff. It is direct information which is true enough at a literal level but it is also being used with satirical intent to say, 'You don't scare me'. But the original line has something else. We can only say it is poetry, and great poetry at that. It defies analysis and is perceived by the right brain.

So, you should know that you are not going to *understand* the material of the next few paragraphs in the way in which you normally expect to understand things, even though it may make a certain amount of sense to your left brain. Try to put your left brain on 'hold' for a while and allow your right brain to 'get' what I am saying in the way that it 'got' (or did not get) the poetry in Othello's words. It is really a matter of allowing the material to be there, suspending judgements on it and taking what you get from it. We are not going to go very deeply into these issues, just sketch the outlines of them.

The astrologer cannot synthesize a chart in the sense in which we are using the term in this book. Only the client can do that by having the information become real for him and using it to discover what is actually so about himself. (I will use the expression 'what is so' rather than 'the truth' because it is not so loaded.) What an astrologer *can* do is create circumstances which facilitate the client making the synthesis. To create such circumstances does not require a degree in psychology or an understanding of complex theories: it requires a grasp of the principle that lies at the root of a technology of personal change or enlightenment.

The principle, expanded a little, is this. All we need to move on from the problems that engulf us is to see clearly what is so about them, to accept them non-judgementally, and to assume responsibility for them. It does not make left-brain sense to say that we are responsible for, or intend to have, our problems. The left brain thinks that they were imposed on us, that we have to fight and struggle against them. The right brain knows that they are part of an evolving pattern, a never-ceasing dance of creation, maintenance and destruction. (Your left brain probably does not know what I am talking about. Keep it on hold for a while longer.)

In order to release ourselves from the processes that run us we need first to become clear about them, second to accept them in a non-judgemental way, and third to assume that we created them. When we do that with a particular process, it completes itself and we automatically move on to something else. Living successfully is simply a matter of 'being here now' and that is very difficult to do.

It is no good believing in this three-part principle (an intellectual position). We have to *experience* the truth of it with our right brain before we can use it effectively with clients. Fortunately, it does not take more than a small amount of experience to start with, otherwise none of us would ever get anywhere. Some people seem to have big life-changing revelations but for most of us it is like peeling an onion — we can only do it a bit at a time.

We will now switch back to normal left-brain working! Astrology fits into this three-part process in the first stage. Often people are completely unconscious of the patterns that run them. They may say they know themselves and believe that they do but what they mean is that they are familiar with their habitual thoughts and attitudes, their likes and dislikes and certain of their reactions. For example, it is quite possible to go through life knowing, at one level, that you always react to the prospect of meeting new people with stagefright, no matter how often you do it, yet never link it with broader patterns that underlie the stagefright. In the interests of day-to-day functioning you can gloss over the stagefright, and never really confront it.

Astrology is such a powerful tool for diagnosis that it can mirror accurately the psychological patterns that make up a person's life. Indeed an astrological session should hold up a mirror to the client so that he can take a look at himself. Whether he will recognize the image is another matter. In some ways, it is perhaps a better analogy to compare an interpreted chart with an X-ray photograph. Most people who see an X-ray photograph of themselves will not know how to read it. They will be able to recognize the broad outlines of certain structures but will not know what to look for beyond that. Using astrology as a counselling tool to help a client synthesize the material and use it to make a difference in his life can be compared with training him to read the X-ray (which of course means that you have to be able to do it yourself).

We need to look, again briefly, at the practical issues involved in counselling and we first need to be clear about what counselling is. In some ways, it is easier to say what counselling is not. It is not interpreting a chart and giving advice. Some astrologers do that and say they are doing counselling, especially if they interpret the chart in some psychological depth. There is nothing wrong with working this way and, in any case, it is what a great many clients will want and expect. It is not counselling, though. Terms like 'chart reading' or 'consultation' can be used for the kind of work that is basically concerned with giving accurate information. An astrologer working in this way is not essentially different from any other kind of information giver, such as an investment adviser.

Counselling involves working with the entire astrologer/chart/client system. It is not giving cut and dried information to the client. It is a joint process of discovery, with the astrologer and client operating in more or less equal partnership. The kind of work that I have called 'chart reading' is working with the chart only: it involves the client very little and the astrologer even less.

The essential characteristic of counselling is that the astrologer should create a safe space for the client to explore what is so for him. To do this, we have to be willing for the client to be the way he is and to give up our own need to be right. This is not easy in any circumstances — it can be especially difficult for the astrologer who often feels insecure not only about his interpretation skills but about the validity of astrology itself. This is why I raised the metaphysical questions about the nature of astrology in Chapter 1. They need to be confronted and made peace with or they will get in the way of effective counselling. If we are not clear about them, it will be very difficult not to cling to being right about some position we hold about astrology. Similarly we need to be confident of our interpretational skills, including our ability to organize the chart material in the ways which we have been discussing in this book.

The second rule of counselling is to listen to what the client says. This means not only hearing the words but perceiving the attitudes and feelings that underlie them. Pay attention to the client's body language. Is it relaxed and open or is it tightly crunched up, with folded arms, crossed legs and hunched shoulders? As far as possible, stay in a relaxed and open body position yourself, even if you are feeling nervous. Put your own feelings and reactions on hold — both your reactions to what the client is saying and your internal ones, such as nervousness. Don't pretend the reactions are not there; acknowledge them and choose to keep your attention on the client. Above all do not sit there waiting for the client to finish speaking so that you can rush in with some piece of interpretation from the chart and *explain* what he has been saying!

We can help clients most simply by listening to what they have to say and really registering it in our own experience. It does not sound like much but it can produce some kind of magic that enables clients to get a different perspective on their issues — maybe only slightly different, but enough for them to begin to move away from whatever fixed position they held.

In this type of counselling, the information from the chart is used to provoke discussion, to push the client's buttons so that you can jointly examine the mechanisms that are activated. The reason we spent so much time in earlier chapters on organizing the chart information into about half a dozen or so major themes is that this is the form in which it is most effective for button-pushing.

Armed with a list of the themes, backed up by the basic notes, we are in a position to give our full attention to interacting with the client. The interpretation part of the job has been done. It should not present any pitfalls or spring any nasty surprises during the course of the session.

We need to begin the session with some kind of introduction, such as briefly discussing the principles of discovering what is so and accepting it. The client does not have to *agree* with these principles, but he does have to be aligned with them. He needs, as it were, to be willing to play the game by those rules for the duration of the session and at least give them some room in his life afterwards. The object of the session is first of all to have the client discover how the themes actually manifest in his life. Whether we go through them and discuss them one by one or read them all out straight off and come back to things that seem important depends on the client's reactions and our own 'feel' of the session.

In any event, we should read out one or all of the themes to the client and explain that they are approximations. They may not operate in his life exactly as they are worded but they should be close enough to ring some bells. We can ask the client if they do make sense and invite him to talk about how they actually manifest in his or her life. My own preference is to start with a theme that I think the client will recognize easily and feel unthreatened by — in terms of subpersonalities, one that is likely to be a member of the 'central club'. With the Auden chart, for example, I would choose the first theme to start with — the emphasis on communicating and learning, being gregarious and talkative. I would expect him to respond to this one and talk about it quite freely, without there being any particular emotional charge on it. By the same token, I would not expect it to push any buttons that we could usefully work with. The point of doing this, of course, is to give clients confidence in your interpretation of the chart and to get them talking about themselves. Once they have got into the swing of talking about how the chart actually manifests in their lives, they are more likely to be willing to do the same with material that does have an emotional charge.

I would not go so far as to elevate the principle of 'start with an easy one' into an absolute rule. Every counselling session is unique.

At the same time, we will not go far wrong if we follow it as a general guide. It is essential, in this kind of work, to create a *rapport* and moving into the session gently is a good way of doing it. The only circumstances I can think of where plunging straight in to one of the more difficult themes might be appropriate is when the client is someone we already know on a fairly intimate basis. However, this will very rarely be the case. Apart from anything else, it is difficult to work in this way with someone we know well in other contexts since the other aspects of the relationship tend to intrude on the session.

Perhaps the first two or three themes may be discussed at some length without any major issues being activated. Eventually, though, something will come up which is a stumbling block in the client's life. This is what you need to encourage him to talk about. What is important is that he should become aware of the concrete, specific way in which the theme manifests in his life and that he should feel the feelings that go with it. The extent to which he does this will determine how far he moves on from the issue. It will become genuine self-knowledge, not merely information to be forgotten in a few days or even hours.

No doubt this account I have given of the process sounds very simplistic. I have said nothing, for example, about the various ways in which the clients will unconsciously resist seeing what is so for them. I have tried in one chapter to give an over-view of material that requires at least two or three books. It has only been possible here to give some very general pointers to a way of working with astrology that goes beyond the bald giving of information and enables the synthesis to take place.

Since this kind of counselling involves the entire astrologer/chart/client system it follows that the astrologer must be willing constantly to explore his own problems and patterns and tell the truth about what is so for him in his own life. This is a major commitment and one that it is not easy to withdraw from. I have no doubt that many readers will feel that they prefer to continue to use astrology at the level of information giving. I hope they will find the material in the main part of the book useful.

For those who wish to explore further the possibilities of astrological counselling — and thereby further explore themselves — I can offer no set programme. To a large extent, it is a matter of seeing what kinds of information and experiences are available and making use of those which suit your own approach. What I can suggest is a reading list (see p. 141) which should point you in your own right direction. In the end, we all have to create our own form of counselling, even though it may bear a strong resemblance to someone else's or be derived from many sources.

READING LIST

ASTROLOGY

Roy Alexander. *The Astrology of Choice*, York Beach: Samuel Weiser (1983).
Christina Rose. *Astrological Counselling*, Wellingborough: Aquarian Press (1982).
Both these books deal specifically with counselling and with astrological symbolism and meanings in some detail.

Stephen Arroyo. *Astrology, Karma and Transformation*, California: CRCS (1978).
Liz Greene. *Saturn*, New York: Samuel Weiser (1976).
Robert Hand. *Horoscope Symbols*, Massachusetts: Para Research (1981).
'Jinni and Joanne'. *The Spiral of Life*, Seattle: Search (1974).
Betty Lundsted. *Astrological Insights into Personality*, San Diego: Astro Computing Services (1980).
Dane Rudhyar. *The Practice of Astrology*, Colorado: Shambala (1968).
Joanne Wickenburg. *A Journey through the Birth Chart*, Seattle: Search (1981).
All these books will help deepen your understanding of astrology and improve your interpretation skills.

PSYCHOLOGY, PSYCHOTHERAPY AND PHILOSOPHY

Eric Berne. *What Do You Say After You Say Hello?*, New York: Bantam (1972).
Claude Steiner. *Scripts People Live*, New York: Grove Press (1974).
Both these books are about transactional analysis.

Marilyn Ferguson. *The Aquarian Conspiracy*, London: Granada (1982).

Eugene T. Gendlin. *Focusing*, New York: Bantam (1981).
A powerful, do-it-yourself method of learning to discover and be with what is so about you. Highly recommended for experiential work.

Piero Ferrucci. *What We May Be*, Wellingborough: Turnstone Press (1982).
Theories and techniques of psychosynthesis.

Arthur Janov. *Prisoners of Pain*, London: Abacus (1980).
An account of how basic fear, anxiety and pain are built up.

Alexander Lowen. *Fear of Life*, New York: Collier Books (1980).
This book is about Bioenergetics, a method of learning to re-experience one's body.

Luke Rhinehart. *The book of* est, London: Abacus (1976).
A fictional re-creation of the famous 'enlightenment experience'.

Ron Smothermon. *Winning Through Enlightenment*, San Francisco: Context Publications (1980).

THE BRAIN: RIGHT AND LEFT HEMISPHERES

Betty Edwards. *Drawing on the Right Side of the Brain*, Glasgow: Fontana (1982).
As its title implies, this book is about learning to draw. The exercises in it give a powerful experience of the existence of the right and left hemispheres of the brain. (At least they do if you can't draw, as I can't — or my left brain can't!)

INDEX